FIVE BODIES

Paul Klee, "Leaning." Copyright 1985 ADAGP, Montreal.

FIVE BODIES

The Human Shape of Modern Society

John O'Neill

Cornell University Press

ITHACA AND LONDON

First published 1985 by Cornell University Press.

International Standard Book Number 0–8014–1727–9
Library of Congress Catalog Card Number 84-22947
Printed in the United States of America
Librarians: Library of Congress cataloging information
appears on the last page of the book.

The paper in this book is acid-free and meets the guidelines for
permanence and durability of the Committee on Production Guidelines
for Book Longevity of the Council on Library Resources.

FOR MY SISTER, JOAN

CONTENTS

ACKNOWLEDGMENTS

Since 1972 my undergraduate students enrolled in a course on the sociology of the body have listened while I tried to shape a varying and often bewildering body of information into something like the corpus of knowledge I now offer after so much patient typing by my secretaries Evelyn Greenberg and Rose Kaminski of Founders College. My manuscript has been considerably improved in clarity and style by Kay Scheuer of Cornell University Press. I also gratefully acknowledge the use of Jonathan Miller's film series and book, *The Body in Question* (London: Jonathan Cape, 1978). On alternative weeks Miller showed us the difference between our two bodies in the history and practice of medicine while I was stuck with the purely verbal arts that explore the communicative body. Nevertheless, it would be nice to think that between Miller's use of open bodies and my exploration of the body's symbolic surfaces we have together contributed to that great university of the open mind.

Five Bodies assumed something like its present form when I was invited to present the argument in the Department of Psychology at the University of Dallas, Texas, in 1980. Earlier versions of particular chapters were tried out between 1972 and 1982 in lectures and seminars given at the following universities: in Canada—McMaster University, Queen's University, and

Concordia University; in England—the London School of Economics and Political Science and the Institute of Contemporary Arts; in Europe—the American College in Paris, the University of Geneva, the University of Louvain, the University of Groningen, and the University of Milan. I am grateful to them all. Finally, in the United States, it is a pleasure to recall visits to the University of South Florida, the State University of New York at Buffalo, Michigan State University, Ithaca College, St. John's University, and the Ohio State University. I also thank my own home, York University, where I am free to think as I do, as well as my family—Maria, Daniela, Gregory, and Brendan, whose love and intelligence are also written here.

J. O'N.

THE PROSTHETIC GOD

No ONE has done more than Freud to explore the costs of inscribing civilization upon our bodies. When he stood back to contemplate civilization and its discontents, Freud could not envisage the new bioprosthetics that would once again open the civilizational frontier, creating new powers and new dependencies in us. Humankind has wrapped itself in a science and technology whose omnipotence has delivered us from our childhood into a certain if uncomfortable divinity. As Freud remarked: "Man has, as it were, become a kind of prosthetic god. When he puts on all his auxiliary organs he is truly magnificent; but these organs have not grown on him and they still give him trouble at times."[1] In the following chapters, I stand at some distance from Freud's conception of the infantile nature of the first humans and their gods, and so I am less inclined to abuse them with the faults of our modern technological fixation. Rather, I am concerned to rethink the civic legacy bequeathed to us in the *sociopoetics* of the first humans, whose families and gods have survived most of the history of our own inhumanity and are still alive in the most ordinary places of mankind. If we have anything to fear from humanity's capacity for metamorphosis, it is from the aweful potential we now have to erase all other living forms along with ourselves. The truly unthinkable

11

side of our civilizational discontent is that we may well be the first human society to think of itself as the *last*. Before such a prospect, we are obliged to rethink the human body, to reconstitute its family, its political economy, and its biotechnologies. Such a task cannot be indifferent to us, as the women of Greenham Common testify to this day, as the young men and women of the world call upon the old men to recognize before it is too late. If the old men do not awaken from their extraterrestrial fantasies, we shall not be lucky enough even to leave behind us any marked grave and certainly no child of our civilization, nor any gods.

JOHN O'NEILL

Toronto

FIVE BODIES

OUR TWO BODIES

Anthropomorphism. Attribution of human form or character.
a. Ascription of a human form and attributes to the Deity.
b. Ascription of a human attribute or personality to
   anything impersonal or irrational.
                                    —*Oxford English Dictionary*

I PROPOSE, despite the dictionary, that human beings
cannot do without the practice of anthropomorphism. If they
were to refrain from it entirely, the world would assume a character more alien than that of any deity. Therefore anthropomorphism is an essential human response; it is a creative force
in the human shaping of human beings and of their civil and
divine institutions. It is a conceit of logicians that we could think
otherwise. Yet, how dare I reinvent anthropomorphism? Even
if I am not afraid of fallacy, oughtn't I to respect intellectual fashion? Man does not belong in his own creation—any more than
God. This may seem odd but, so we are told, it is better looked
upon as an exciting opportunity—supposing we survive the in-
vitation to social and moral chaos. We do, more or less. But I
think we do it by living off borrowed moral capital. Therefore I
want to raise the old question: who makes man? This is the anthropomorphic question. By asking it and in looking for responses to it we make ourselves human.

It is essential for us to proceed in this way. We cannot other-

15

wise establish the radical grounds of an anthropomorphizing social science. The loss of the human in the social and literary sciences meets with equal lament and celebration. The progress of human knowledge seems to require the abandonment of an anthropocentric or human-centered world-view—a proposition I do not seriously challenge. It has become clear, however, that in the process people have lost the power to give a human shape to human institutions, a power I think is the radical core of an anthropomorphizing perspective in the social sciences that we must revive if we are to defend ourselves against the equal excesses of subjective and subjectless science. Moreover, I believe that the vital issues in the complex relation between persons, nature, and social institutions may well be approached through our unavoidable interest in the human body. We shall see in some detail how the human body is an intelligent and critical resource in the anthropomorphic production of those small and larger orders that underlie our social, political, and economic institutions. Such an argument is at first sight far from obvious, since the body is generally regarded as something either far too intimate or else far too unruly to be the starting place for a study of the intelligent order in our public lives. It seems odd, for example, to speak of a "sociology" or of a *political economy of the body*. The body would surely seem to lie outside the concerns of sociology, economics, and politics as these disciplines are generally understood. But to the extent this is so, much of what we ordinarily know and feel about our lives and the quality of our public life is ignored.

The Physical Body and the Communicative Body

In what sense do we understand the body that enters into our social life? It is sometimes thought that the body is a physical object like other objects that stand around us. As such, our *physical body* can be bumped into, knocked over, crushed, and destroyed. Yet, even as we say this, our language is estranged or alienated from the *lived body*, that is, that communicative bodily presence to which we cannot be indifferent, to which we are as sensible in others as in ourselves.[1] Because of the inseparability of these two bodies, we treat even the physical body as a *moral body* to which we owe respect, help, and care, and for whose injuries we are responsible even in our own person. Moreover, society strongly sanctions the protection of bodies. Those who inflict deliberate injury upon others risk incarceration and other bodily harms, and even those who are merely clumsy risk at least embarrassment, if not moral condemnation. Thus, even the physical body is, morally speaking, more than a simple object for biological study or medical practice and may in fact require us to rethink their procedures: witness the reinvention of holistic medicine. In any case, we cannot treat the anatomy and physiology of the body as paradigmatic of what persons are required to know about bodily conduct and comportment in social settings. The *communicative body* we learn to think and have is the general medium of our world, of its history, culture, and political economy. Maurice Merleau-Ponty wrote:

> The body is our general medium for having a world. Sometimes it is restricted to the actions necessary for the conservation of life, and accordingly it posits around us a biological world; at other times, elaborating upon these primary actions and moving from their literal to a figurative meaning, it manifests through them a core of new significance: this is true of motor habits such as dancing. Sometimes, finally, the meaning aimed at cannot be achieved by the body's natural means; it must then build itself an instrument, and it projects thereby around itself a cultural world.[2]

The preceding distinctions are not meant to diminish the importance in our lives of the biological body. I mean only to deepen the connections between biology and culture which arise precisely because the human body is a communicative body whose upright posture and audiovisual articulation opens up a symbolic world that enriches our experience beyond any other form of life.[3] We never experience those aspects of the body I have differentiated as the physical body and the communicative body except as a unity comprising incredible variety, depending on historical and social circumstances. Societies have come to no universal agreements about the proper ritualization of the bodily experiences of birth, death, pain, pleasure, hunger, fear, beauty, and ugliness. How, then, are we to regard the body as a topic of inquiry for social science rather than as the object solely of biomedical science? What is to be learned about the body that could possibly aid us in our understanding of the larger issues of social order, conflict, and change? Even if there were anything to be learned, how would it be of more than passing interest? Surely, science is in pursuit of order, regularity, and generalizations that are independent of bodily behavior? Generally speaking, sociology is the study of the rules and normative behavior that proceed from people's beliefs and not from their bodily chemistry or physiology. Therefore, it will be said, *society is in our minds, not in our bodies.* Such, at any rate, might be concluded from centuries of religious, philosophical, and educational practice. We conceive of public order dualistically, that is to say, as the rule of mind over matter, or of reason over the senses. In this view, our bodies are the unwilling servants of the moral and intellectual order. Thus we need to discipline our bodies to achieve excellence, to enter heaven, or to endure the passivity of sitting in a lecture hall to gather the good news of sociology,[4] let alone to read this book!

It is not an easy task to understand how social institutions rethink the body.[5] It is even more difficult to understand how *we can rethink institutions with our bodies.* But this is what we shall be doing in this book. Recently, Michel Foucault has brought to our attention the difficult notion that, far from repressing the body, modern political economy exercises power over it by opening up, so to speak, the *sexual* body as a discursive channel into which we confess endlessly who we are and what we desire:

> Sexuality must not be described as a stubborn drive, by nature alien and of necessity disobedient to a power which exhausts itself trying to subdue it and often fails to control it entirely. It appears rather as an especially dense transfer point for relations of power:

between men and women, young people and old people, parents and offspring, teachers and students, priests and laity, an administration and a population. Sexuality is not the most intractable element in power relations, but rather one of those endowed with the greatest instrumentality: useful for the greatest number of maneuvers and capable of serving as a point of support, as a linchpin, for the most varied strategies.[6]

I think it is necessary to keep in mind that the reduction of the communicative body to the sexual body is a historical process that distorts the gendered cosmology that governed nature, society and the human body, subordinating it to the industrialization of nature and the human family, which we shall discuss in later chapters.[7] Thus I have reconstructed this history in terms of what I call the shift from history as *biotext* to history as *sociotext* (see the conclusion), and this provides the frame upon which the following chapters hang. At the same time, I wish to take a radical stand against antihumanism and, in particular, against any fashionable credo of *defamilization*, whose aim is to strengthen the state and the market as the ultimate matrix of human life.[8] I reject this last phase of neo-individualism. Rather, I think with Vico that it is inconceivable that we could ever constitute society in the will to contract all human relations outside of the great historical body of our family and its society. Here, then, I appeal to *a familied history without which there cannot be any one of us*. The telling of that history goes beyond the confessional practices of today's advice columns as much as it does our official historical writing. It cannot be divided into the history of great men, nor can it be assigned to the new histories of women and children. Each of us keeps this familied history and in all things we are a witness to it. For it is holy. In the words of Gertrude Stein:

> A history of any one must be a long one, slowly it comes out of them from their beginning to their ending, slowly you can see it in them the nature and the mixtures in them, slowly everything comes out from each one in the kind of repeating each one does in the different parts and kinds of living they have in them, slowly

then the history of them comes out from them, slowly then any one who looks well at any one will have the history of the whole of that one. Slowly the history of each one comes out of each one. Sometime then there will be a history of every one.[9]

The Communicative Body

Today we witness a growing movement in post-industrial societies to redefine bodily experience as nothing more than sheer labor power, to be managed as the docile instrument of commercial, educational, and medical practice. To come to terms with such a movement, we must critically rethink the analytic practices of economics, politics, medicine, and the social sciences, a process that we shall look at in the following chapters. What makes such examinations difficult, thereby retarding the social and political changes to which they might contribute, is that social scientists tend to study disembodied persons, preferring to work with quantitative data or interview schedules. It is the function of much sociological discourse to enact a ritual of decontamination between the scientist and his subject. It is essential that the professional sociologist resist the look in the eyes of the sick, the poor, and the aimless who turn his questions back upon him. Through the interview schedule or attitude survey the embodied subject is plucked clean. As the sociological apparatus increases in size and complexity, it has to be housed in offices and institutes and its services can be afforded only by wealthy clients. It also demands standards of decorum from the sociologist which make it difficult for him (because of dress, language, and sensibility) to pass in the underworld of crime, sex, race, and poverty. The professional sociologist is curiously caught in his own caste.[10]

It is essential that we social scientists remind ourselves of the fundamentally communicative body that is the moral basis of all society and of the practice of any social science. We cannot escape life among others. Our bodies commit us from the first moment of life to the company of those who have grown up and who, in turn, oblige themselves to care for our physical well-being. Of course, the aim of the care we receive as children is to bring us to care for ourselves, to free us from the dependency of an immature body and an uneducated mind. Thus the satisfaction of our bodily needs is never intended by those who care for us to yield in us a merely selfish pleasure. Human care initiates us into a *tradition of caring* whereby we learn to give back what we ourselves have received. This is an essential condition of society.[11] Unless it is realized, we are threatened with the prospect of a society—which I examine later—where there is no genuine sociability, but merely the exchange of selfish and calculated interests between individuals who sense no deeper bond among them. Rather, sociability rests upon our reciprocal experience and upon the vulnerability and openness to one another that arises from the kind of communicative life we enjoy as embodied beings.

Our bodies, then, are the fine instruments of both the smaller and the larger society in which we live. Human dexterity is such that we are capable of an infinitely wide use of tools which in turn feed in and out of the huge divisions of labor that are the basis of society in its broadest sense. Our bodies are also the warm instrument of the most intimate associations we know. In particular, we make special use of our bodies to celebrate our sheer sociability whenever we dress, adorn our necks, arms, wrists, and eyes, paint our cheeks and lips, or exchange smiles, kisses, and handshakes. Thus, whenever our bodies are unwell, we generally beg off parties and social gatherings, just as our general commitment to sociability requires otherwise weight-conscious people to eat and drink on behalf of others, with mild protests, more than is good for themselves. If the body is the instrument of our commitment to various types of social engagements and tasks, it is also the instrument of our refusal of society on particular occasions and in specific ways. Small children will scream and kick, refuse to eat or sleep, make a mess, and get themselves dirty to express their dislike for parental wishes. Prisoners and psychiatric patients, not to mention adolescents, will do the same. Here the body is the instrument of refusal and rejection, just as from the standpoint of authority its compliance is the instrument of order.[12] Hence the ultimate social sanction is incarceration, confining the body, and submitting it to pain, torture, hunger, and perhaps even execution. Revolutionaries, rebels, heretics, delinquents, criminals, and even the sick all risk their bodies in some way as the price of contesting society's official bodies and their established practices.

We are continuously caught up and engaged in *the embodied look of things*, especially in the look of others and of ourselves. Although philosophers and moralists have decried our attachment to appearances and superficialities, as sociologists we cannot ignore the elaborate social construction of embodied appearances in which we are necessarily engaged as persons. Indeed, it is here that we touch upon two very basic aspects of our social life. It is through our senses that we first appreciate and evaluate others, immediately shaping our own positive, pleasurable, and trusting responses, or else our negative, fearful, and avoiding reactions. What we see, hear, and feel of other persons is the first basis for our interaction with them. This is the carnal ground of our social knowledge. Because *society is never a disembodied spectacle*, we engage in social interaction from the very start on the basis of sensory and aesthetic impressions. The look of the other person is the prima facie ground of our knowledge of him or her. We do not engage from the start in endless doubts about whether appearances are deceiving. As embodied persons, whose needs are not easily suspended, we are obliged for all practical purposes to treat appearances as realities. Merleau–Ponty points out: "Saying that I have a body is thus a way of saying that I can be seen as an object and that I try to be seen as a subject, that another can be my master or my slave, so that shame and shamelessness express the dialectic of the plurality of consciousness, and have a metaphysical significance."[13]

We seek out other bodies in society as mirrors of ourselves—the second basic feature of social life. And this is because our own bodies are the permeable ground of all social behavior; our bodies are the very flesh of society. Charles Horton Cooley spoke of this permeable ground in nearly bodily terms when he drew the attention of sociologists and psychologists to the notion of the *looking glass self*.[14] What we see in the mirror is what others see. Here is *the incarnate bond between self and society*. What sociologists call the socialization process, namely, the bringing up of an infant or child by those who care for it in accordance with the prevailing standards of behavior, rests upon the infant's *visceral knowledge* of what is required of it, conveyed as early as its feeding, cuddling, handling, toileting experiences with its mother. From its earliest moments, and long before it can apprentice to the rules of perception, language, and conduct, the child's body resonates with its social experience. The warm community of the child's world "somehow"—being precise would require a psychoanalysis—stands as our first world, the measure of all our other worldly engagements. What Cooley called the "looking glass self" is actually part of the complex acquisition of what is now called the *body image*, which involves passing through a crucial *mirror stage* that enables the infant to become aware of the distinction between its experience of its *own body* and the other person's experience of it as *a body*.[15] Thus from infancy we acquire the ability to mirror our intentions in the facial and linguistic expressions of the mother as the prima facie basis for their further elaboration according to the mother's sense of their meaning.

Since human embodiment functions to create the most fundamental bond between the self and society, we might now briefly look at some of its consequences in settings of adult life that may at first sight seem strange or trivial and yet be of enormous consequence in the lives of those committed to the embodied universe of social appearances. No society seems content to leave the biophysical body outside the symbolic system whereby members communicate to one another their age, gender, marital status, sexual availability, social standing, and the like.[16] It is in this light that we can understand that the elaborate cosmetic and grooming practices in which persons of all sorts are involved for a considerable amount of the day, at enormous cost and by means of the strangest of rituals, are a necessary expression of their commitment to prevailing social mores and values. We must think of the detail of such practices as body painting, scarification, adornment, hair-cutting and dressing, washing, perfuming, deodorizing, covering and concealing various bodily parts, as a resource for the incessant *eye-work*[17] whereby we make the way people appear constituent features of social reality. Thus, a good deal of the information we need in order to be properly oriented in the social settings in which we find ourselves is visually available in the form of *body advertisements* practiced by the most ordinary persons, and only accentuated by models. It is important, then, to connect the otherwise bewildering variety of these techniques of the body to the two basic functions of embodiment and the social self we have previously discussed. Moreover, it cannot be sufficiently stressed how these bodily readings represent massive, vulgarly available competences whose work achieves an *incarnate society*, that is, the embodied reality of everyday life.

Of course, our carnal knowledge of embodied persons is always defeasible in the light of our further experience with them. And, as we find ourselves in situations further and further away from intimate, friendly, and familial relations—not that these cannot be hard to disentangle—we need to acquire a larger sense of institutional and role requirements in order to make sense of the behavior around us and what it requires on our part. Sociologists generally confine themselves to the analysis of behavior and interaction in large institutional settings for which they provide cognitive maps whose virtuosity is undeniable. But, at many points, sociological descriptions of institutional settings are essentially and irreparably abstract because they fail to provide for social agents as embodied persons, engaged in embodied inquiries. In everyday life, however, we have—and must have—society in our bones, so to speak. The work of institutions is finely grained into our physical, mental, nervous, and moral constitution—and this is what accomplishes the daily marvel of social order with its pleasures and pains, its rewards and punishments.

24

Because the general practice of the social sciences belongs to the administrative strategies of modern society, it is necessary to correct its organizational bias in favor of those moral bodies it claims to serve. Increasingly, we fear that modern organizations are the life-machines to which the moral body is hooked up by every sort of bureaucratic tape. It is in order to resist the drift toward a *mechano-morphic or prosthetic society* in which the ordinary intelligence and sensibililty of persons are rendered docile and passive, that we turn to the study of the fundamental competences of the communicative body in shaping our cosmology, some contemporary institutions, and the future shape of human beings.

CHAPTER ONE

THE WORLD'S BODY

MODERN humans are busy giving a shape to a world that is no longer their own. Such, at any rate, is the complaint of many artists and social scientists who speak of our world alienation, or as I see it, a process of *negative anthropomorphism*. We are no longer reflected in our work, our institutions, or our environment. The abstraction of modern experience is based upon the removal of the human shape in favor of the measured—number, line, sign, code, index. Everywhere anthropomorphism, the creative force in the human shaping of human beings, is in retreat. Such a fate would be unthinkable were it not in fact intelligible as a strategy whereby humankind has redesigned its own body, its family, the body politic, the economy, nature and the universe in order to exercise a form of domination over the world and itself that threatens to be the last of all metamorphoses. At the same time, there are indications that, despite our unprecedented power over the universe and ourselves, we still feel the need for the bond of affection, the ties of local community, and for the familiar resonance of our own kind in smaller worlds of ordinary things fitted more cosily, even if more shabbily, to the human frame.

The decline of anthropomorphism represents a huge shift in our cosmography. Whereas formerly people could think the universe through their bodies and their own bodies through the universe—each to each a model of totality, and proportion—today they must think systems and structures without embodied subjects. Just as robots do the work in science-fiction systems, so, we are to believe, literary systems do the work of artists confined now to clever ventriloquy no better than that of the official language which subordinates social life to bureaucratic systems. In all modern systems we abstract from embodiment, time and, community.[1] The promise is that these embodied limits of the human polity will be transcended, or else marginalized, in the release of collective energy and control exercised through imaginative science fictions whose power lies in their ability to deal with evolutionary levels of complexity and openness beyond the scope of anthropomorphic thought.

I do not mean to reject nonanthropocentric science. Rather, my purpose is to keep alive the ground from which science starts and to which its promise is beholden. I shall argue, therefore, that *the ground of universal science is the world's body*.[2] It might be claimed that anthropomorphism is only *faute de mieux* the source of primitive peoples' cosmology. I would rather argue with Vico that the rationalist reconstruction of the cosmos is possible only on the ground of that first *poetic logic* whereby people thought the world with their bodies: "The human mind is naturally inclined by the senses to see itself externally in the body, and only with great difficulty does it come to understand itself by means of reflection. This axiom gives us the universal principle of etymology in all languages: words are carried over from bodies and from the properties of bodies to signify the institutions of the mind and spirit."[3]

The magnificent insight in Vico's *New Science* is that human society could not have been created from the start according to rationalist principles. Rather, Vico, like Durkheim much later, saw that primitive people necessarily thought the world with their gendered bodies, or with their families, since these and not the mind are the ground of all rational categories. Modern science can hardly overestimate the importance of the legacy of primitive cosmological thought. It is impossible to imagine an unmapped universe waiting for the rationalist sciences to domesticate it. Our ancestors would more likely have died from fear had they not from the very beginning anthropomorphized and thereby domesticated everything around them. The distance between the categorial schemas of modern science and those of our early ancestors is tiny compared with the inconceivable gap between a world anthropomorphized and sheer chaos. In short, it is the very continuity between modern and primitive thought that was guaranteed when our ancestors thought the world in terms of their gendered bodies and families. As Durkheim and Mauss observe: "The first logical categories were social categories; the first classes were classes of men, into which things were integrated. It was because men were grouped, and thought of themselves in the form of groups, that in their ideas they grasped other things, and in the beginning the two modes of groupings were merged to the point of being indistinct. Moieties were the first genera; clans the first species. Things were thought to be integral parts of society, and it was their place in society which determined their place in nature."[4]

Thus human beings think nature and society with their bodies. That is to say, they first think the world and society as one giant body. In turn, the divisions of the body yield the divisions of the world and of society, of humans and of animals. Primitive classification, therefore, followed an *embodied logic* of division of gender and kinship and replication, which, far from being unscientific or irrational, was the very foundation on which later, abstract and rationalized modes of categorization could be developed in both the human and the natural sciences. It can be argued, therefore, that the rational class concepts are not simply a unilinear development from the first imaginative universals but that both are structural elements of an inseparable historical and social matrix. The myths of the first people are not the poor science of modern men: nor are they mere allegories or poetic embellishments of truths otherwise achieved by science. They are the indispensable origins of human order and commonwealth apart from which the later achievements of humanism and scientism are impossible conceits. In other words, anthro-pomorphism—and not rationalism—is the necessary first stage of the human world. Vico tells us:

It is noteworthy that in all languages the greater part of the expres-sions relating to inanimate things are formed by metaphor from the human body and its parts and from the human senses and passions. Thus, head for top or beginning; the brow and shoul-ders of a hill; the eyes of needles and of potatoes; mouth for any opening; the lip of a cup or pitcher; the teeth of a rake, a saw, a comb; the beard of wheat; the tongue of a shoe; the gorge of a river; a neck of land; an arm of the sea; the hands of a clock; heart for center (the Latins used *umbilicus*, navel, in this sense); the belly of a sail; foot for end or bottom; the flesh of fruits; a vein of rock or mineral; the blood of grapes for wine; the bowels of the earth. Heaven or the sea smiles; the wind whistles; the waves murmur; a body groans under a great weight. The farmers of Latium used to say the fields were thirsty, bore fruit, were swollen with grain; and our rustics speak of plants making love, vines going mad, resinous trees weeping. Innumerable other examples could be col-lected from all languages. All of which is a consequence of our axiom (120) that man in his ignorance makes himself the rule of the universe, for in the examples cited he has made of himself an entire world. So that, as rational metaphysics teaches that man becomes all things by understanding them (*homo intelligendo fit om-nia*), this imaginative metaphysics shows that man becomes all things by *not* understanding them (*homo non intelligendo fit omnia*); and perhaps the latter proposition is truer than the former, for when man understands he extends his mind and takes in the things, but when he does not understand he makes the things out of himself and becomes them by transforming himself into them.[5]

What Vico conjectured may be seen in the story-shaped world of the Dogon, a West African people who were among the last to come under French colonial rule. Their distance from us should recede as we listen in them to our own need for a story-able world. Indeed, we never go without such stories. Even in today's space fictions what is extra-territorial is really our need of a home and a place for our selves and not only for E.T., as our children recognize.

To the Dogon the world is a great body. It is moreover, a communicative body, and the "word" is the key to everything in the world's body. The Dogon view of the world is anthropomorphic; at every level it reflects the imagery of the gendered body—its minerals and plants, as well as its artifacts, are parts of a gigantic body.[6] The world's body and the world's speech are inseparable. Its story is told to us by Ogotemmêli,[7] once a hunter, now an old and blind villager of Lower Ogol:

Just as the God Amma threw the stars out into space, so he threw from his hand a lump of clay that fell and flattened out in the shape of a woman's body. The anthill is the sexual organ of the world's body and its clitoris is a termite hill. Being lonely, Amma desired the world's body. The termite hill resisted Amma's approaches, and so Amma cut it down. From this disorderly union the jackal was born, a symbol of Amma's difficulties. Thereafter, Amma had further intercourse with his earthwife. Water, the divine seed, entered the earth's womb and so the androgynous twins, Nummo, were born and went to heaven to receive instruction from their father. From there, they saw their mother-earth, naked and speechless. They therefore came down from heaven with the fibers of plants to clothe the earth in a skirt. This was done not only to save her modesty but to restore order through speech. The fibers of the earth's dress were channels of moisture full of Nummo, which is the warm air upon which speech floats. Just as the human body is made up of the elements of water, earth, air and fire, so too is the body of speech. Saliva is water without which speech is dry; air supports the sound of speech; earth gives it its weight and significance, and fire gives speech its warmth. Thus the body's insides are projected outside in the body of speech, each proportioned to the other, like a garment. The Dogon say that to be naked is to be speechless.

The Nummo, however, could see that the descent of the eight original androgynous twins was not secure. They therefore came down again to dwell in the earth's womb. The male

Nummo took the place of the termite-hill clitoris and the female Nummo's womb became part of the earth's womb. In time, the eldest of the ancestor pairs came to the anthill womb occupied by Nummo and sank into it feet first, leaving behind him his food bowl, a symbol of his human body. Inside the earth's womb, he became water and word and then was expelled up into heaven. All eight ancestors went through this metamorphosis. But the seventh ancestor, the symbol of the perfect union of the male element, which is three, and the female element, which is four, was given the mastery of language. This time the language was clearer than the first word that had clothed the earth and was meant for everyone, not just a few initiates. The word of the seventh ancestor contained the progress of the world. He therefore began to occupy the whole of the earth's womb for his purposes. His lips widened to the edge of the anthill which in turn widened so that the earth's womb became a mouth, and pointed teeth appeared to the number of eighty, ten (the number of the fingers) for each ancestor. At sunrise on the appointed day, the seventh ancestor spirit spat out eighty threads of cotton, his upper and lower teeth holding the warp and woof and his whole face working to weave the tissue (text) of the second Word: "The words that the Spirit uttered filled all the interstices of the stuff: they were woven in the threads, and formed part and parcel of the cloth. They were the cloth, and the cloth was the Word. That is why the woven material is called *soy*, which means 'It is the spoken word.' *Soy* also means 'seven,' as the Spirit who spoke as he wove was seventh in the series of ancestors."[8]

It was, however, through the ant that the seventh ancestor passed on the Word, and she in turn relayed it to the men born after the earth had lost her clitoris. Prior to this time, people had lived in simple holes in the earth, like the lairs of animals. They now began to build in the shape of anthills, making rooms with connecting passages, and they began to store food and to mold great teeth of clay around the entrances to their dwellings, like the teeth of the earth's womb: "The ant at the same time revealed the words it had heard and the man repeated them.

31

Thus there was recreated by human lips the concept of life in motion, of the transposition of forces, of the efficacy of the breath of the Spirit, which the seventh ancestor had created; and thus the interlacing of warp and weft enclosed the same words, the new instructions which became the heritage of mankind and was handed on from generation to generation of weavers to the accompaniment of the clapping of the shuttle and the creaking of the block, which they call the 'creaking of the word.'"[9]

Due to a further breach of order in Heaven, the Dogon received the third Word, which is built into the Granary of Pure Earth, the model for all the village granaries. The construction of each granary reflects the elements and stages in the construction of the world. Moreover, its arrangement perfects that of the anthill, which had been the model for humans' first dwellings above ground. The Granary of Pure Earth was built after the shape of a woven basket, with a circular top and square base in which was carried the earth and clay from which the Word was built. This shape was inverted, however, giving the Granary of Pure Earth a circular bottom representing the Sun, and a square top representing the Sky, with a circular opening to represent the Moon. Each of the four sides was cut into by ten steps, the tread of each being female and the riser male. Each of the four sides represented a constellation of animals and stars. The north stairway was for men and fishes; the south stairway was for domestic animals, the east for birds, and the west for wild animals, vegetables, and insects. The granary was entered from the sixth step on the north side, just wide enough to let a man's body pass. This opening was called the mouth of the granary and the rest of the granary was called the world's belly. The interior was divided into four partitioned chambers above and below, numbering eight in all. The eight compartments contained the eight seeds given to the eight ancestors: little millet, white millet, dark millet, female millet, beans, sorrel, rice, and Digitaria. The eight compartments also represented the eight organs of the Spirit of water comparable to human organs, with the addition of the gizzard because the Spirit moves as fast as a bird. The organs were displayed in the following order: stomach, gizzard, heart, small liver, spleen, intestines, great liver, gall bladder. In the center of the granary there stood a round jar, symbolizing the womb; inside, a second smaller jar, containing oil, represented the fetus. On top of the second jar stood an even smaller jar containing perfume, and on this stood two cups: "All the eight organs were held in place by the outer walls and the inner partitions which symbolized the skeleton. The four uprights ending in the corners of the square roof were the arms and legs. Thus the granary was like a woman, lying on her back (representing the sun) with her arms and legs raised and supporting the roof (representing the sky). The two legs were on the north side, and the door at the sixth step marked the sexual parts."[10]

Not only was the Granary of Pure Earth a model of the world's body; it also functioned in its parts to reflect the processes of reproduction, sexually and materially, whereby the world's body renews itself and the Dogon people:

> The granary and all it contained was therefore a picture of the world-system of the new order, and the way in which this system worked was represented by the functioning of the internal organs. These organs absorbed symbolic nourishment which passed along the usual channels of the digestion and the circulation of blood. From compartments 1 and 2 (stomach and gizzard) the symbolical food passed into compartment 6 (the intestines) and from there into all the others in the form of blood and lastly breath, ending in the liver and the gall bladder. The breath is a vapour, a form of water, which maintains and is indeed the principle of life.[11]

The Word of the Dogon, like the seed of the earth's body, is carried in their clavicles, which are called the granary of the little millet, the food that saved the people in times of famine.[12] The clavicles are the guardians of the Dogon's life force, personality, and speech. It is in the water of the clavicles that the sym-

33

bolic grains germinate generating the individual's energy according to his or her rank, role, and activity in the community. The production of speech involves the body working like a smithy: the lungs pumping in and out the air, the heart warming the water. The spleen is the hammer hitting against the stomach; the liver is the anvil; the curved intestine breaks up the food and the words, giving the best to the joints in order to strengthen the body. The uvula represents the smithy's pincers "grasping" the words on the way into the mouth and guiding them out. Having forged the warm moist sounds of speech inside his body, like a blacksmith, the speaker still has to turn these sounds into intelligible speech. The work of giving the sounds their specific and relative character is compared to the work of weaving. The mouth is like a loom weaving intelligible speech suited to all the various occasions, functions, roles, and activities of Dogon life. The nerves of the cranium and the jaws are compared to the rear and front posts that support the loom/mouth, the teeth are the comb, and the tongue the shuttle going back and forth. The throat, actually the vocal chords, is like the pulley that makes the characteristic creak of the loom. The rise and fall of the uvula is compared to the warp and the words themselves to the weaver's threads. The act of speaking—talking, listening, talking—resembles the back-and-forth movements of the hands with the shuttle of the feet moving up and down to alter the height of the threads. The crisscrossing of speech and weaving is also reflected in the continual shift from high to low tones, from female to male sounds, which spell out the endless dialogue of the sexes in the alternating music and dances of the Dogon—just as in the crack of the looms that weave together the Dogon costumes, customs, and community.

Among the Fali of northern Cameroon in West Africa, we also find that the world is organized as a body and that every creature's place and function are described on the analogy of the body parts, functions, and relationships.[13] We cannot follow every aspect of Fali cosmography, but some of its principle elements are worth attention. The universe is divided into four constituent elements, each located as follows:

N

Water

W   Air   Void   Fire   E

Earth

S

To each of these cardinal divisions there are assigned certain colors and mythical animals. Red and the crocodile are placed in the east, white and the toad in the north, light blue and the tortoise in the south, black and the monkey in the center, and the west is compared to the skin of the vanvin, whose mixed coloring resembles the black and white plumage of the guinea fowl. Overall, the east is the region of everything to do with life, force, wealth, fecundity, growth, heat, and knowledge, whereas the west (or north) is the region of weakness, hunger, impotence, cold, ignorance, and death.

The terrestrial world is conceived in terms of an analogous fourfold division of the body and of the Fali themselves. Thus the Kangou group in the east are the head, the Tinguelin in the South are the trunk, the Bossoum in the north are the arms and in the west the Bori-Peske are the outstretched legs of a man lying on his right side and fertilizing the earth—a union at once of male and female, sky and earth. Thus, the world may be represented as a quartet disposed as shown in Illustration I.

In turn, each of the four principal groups is subdivided into four tribes, each correlated with one of the four principal bodily divisions. Superimposed on this quaternary base, we then find a schema for the classification of grains, animals, birds, insects, and the design, contents and functions of the house, all correlated to the bodily schema. Each of these categories is inscribed in the world according to the principal division of the world of the known (human beings, their institutions and activities,

35

N

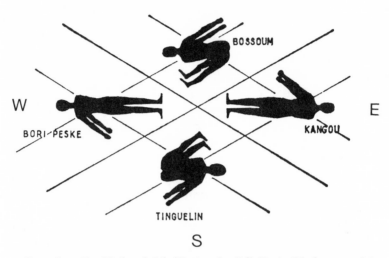

S

1. From Jean-Paul Lebeuf, *L'habitation des Fali* (Paris: Hachette, 1961), p. 437. Copyright © Hachette-Guides Bleus, 1961.

edible grains, and domestic animals) and the unknown world (wild animals, reptiles, birds, insects, and fish).

Among the Tinguelin, then, the world's body looks something like the following:

(1)	Head	(East)	human beings and edible grains
(2)	Chest		the house sheltering the family
		(West)	
(2a)	Stomach		wild animals, birds, fishes, reptiles, everything living in the bush
(3)	Right arm		the fields of millet
		(South)	
(3a)	Left arm		cultivation of ground-nuts

36

(4)	Lower limbs	(North)	the earth in which the edible grains are cultivated

Our ancestors, then, were incredibly inventive in portraying a world in which they had a recognizable place. This, in my opinion, is the same creative impulse that we admire in classical civilization and its legacy to Europe. The continuity of anthropomorphic thought in the West from the pre-Socratics to the Renaissance and in Eastern as well as African and Amerindian societies justifies us in preserving a universal mode of thought essential to our humanity. In other words, I think that anthropomorphism is a potentially radical heritage preserved in our mythology and poetry, reminding us of fundamental ties between the shape of human kind and the shape of society and the universe, each mirrored in the other. As pictured in Plato's *Timaeus*, literate society still thinks itself as a world body containing all other bodies, thereby bringing each of the four families—the heavenly gods (which include the stars, planets, earth), the birds of the air, the fishes of the sea, and the animals on land—closer to one another and to the intelligible Form of the divine Creator. In accordance with this Form, the Demiurge fashions the world's material body, a perfect combination of the four elements held in friendly proportion:

Now the frame of the world took up the whole of each of these four; he who put it together made it consist of all the fire and water and air and earth, leaving no part or power of any one of them outside. This was his intent: first, that it might be in the fullest measure a living being whole and complete, of complete parts; next, that it might be single, nothing left over, out of which such another might come into being; and moreover that it might be free from age and sickness. For he perceived that, if a body be composite, when hot things and cold and all things that have strong powers beset that body and attack it from without, they bring it to untimely dissolution and cause it to waste away by bringing upon it sickness and age. For this reason and so considering, he fashioned it as a single whole consisting of all these wholes, complete and free from age and sickness.[14]

37

It does not demean the *Timaeus* to remark upon its similarity with the myths of Ogotemmêli. The sublimity of their common conception of the world's body makes them comparable. The Demiurge orders chaos with his body, which in turn reflects the order and disorder sown in the universe. The Forms of Truth, Beauty, and Justice are thereby a grounded cosmography precisely because they are written into the body which is "framed like a heaven to include them." Thus the human body is the bridge for all microcosmic and macrocosmic exchanges, as in the Babylonian systems of astrobiology and astrogeography which thrive in our own newspaper and magazine horoscopes. These systems of thought are not to be regarded as the country cousins of psychology and predictive testing. They are, rather, *holy systems*. That is to say, they are concerned with the parallels of wholeness between the planets, the stars, and the human body. As Leonard Barkan explains, the zodiacal and planetary systems pair anatomy and cosmography to give us forecast or freeplay according to our fantasy:

> The planetary system is joined with the human body not astro-nomically, but by the metamorphosis of the planets into gods who have human form and personality. If we carry this system beyond its originally narrow imaginative limits, the Cosmos can form an external stage on which dramas can be acted out and then mir-rored in the working of our anatomy. If we restrict ourselves purely to the plane of anatomy, these dramas are as predictable as all planetary motion; but with the attribution of anthropomorphic significance to the planets via the lives of the gods, the dramas within one human anatomy or among various people have a greater potential field of variety.[15]

A nice depiction of man's astral body and its dramas is to be found in Geoffroy Tory's image of *encyclopedic man* (Illustration 2), whose proportions are identified with the nine muses and the seven liberal arts, and who has the Virtues in his hand and feet. In this image, heaven and earth are harmonized in the hu-mane arts, which in turn repeat a harmony between mind and body, as well as between the individual and society.

38

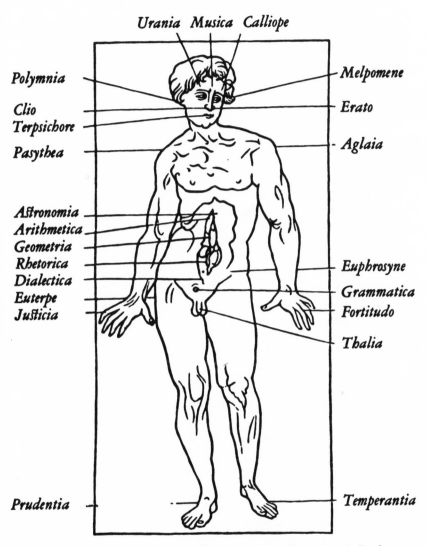

2. Encyclopedic man. From Geoffroy Tory, *Champfleury* (1529), Book II.

The biblical analogy between God's body and man's body generated intricacies of rabbinical scholarship that I will touch on briefly in Chapter 2.[16] The literal and figurative traditions of microcosmography are characteristic of medieval and Renaissance thought. In natural philosophy, theology, mysticism, law, and poetry we constantly find recourse to the body metaphor as a key to the principles of order and hierarchy in man and the universe, and we shall examine something of this in the imagery of the body politic (Chapter 3). How the literal and figurative traditions functioned is succinctly put by Barkan:

> In the literary image of the body as microcosm, the literal and figurative visions are joined; but in the history of natural philosophy through the Middle Ages and the Renaissance, the figurative tradition remained independent from the literal and very much more in the mainstream of thought. The figurative view of man as microcosm arises out of a great variety of philosophical traditions and periods, but it is always composed of two parts: a *method*, the metaphoric imagination that transforms a non-human phenomenon into an equivalent within human experience, and a *content*, the idea that man contains everything which he can perceive in the world around him. These are the presuppositions of humanism, whether classical, medieval, or Renaissance. The method praises man's mind, and the content praises his condition.[17]

Thus in the Renaissance Pico della Mirandola attributed man's glory to his body, believing that it is only man's physiognomy which is freely determinable in respect of heaven and earth. Only man can become an angel or a beast; or, as we might now add, a robot. Every one of these options, however, arises for us only inasmuch as we are uniquely embodied beings. Thereafter, the mind may figuratively contain the whole universe, *homo omnis creatura*. Such is the imagery that fed the religion, science, law, and poetry of the world until Copernicus, Galileo, and Newton displaced anthropomorphic cosmography with modern physics. Then the world's body became remote, a thing indifferent to the human body and to human fables of cosmic in-

fluence. Bacon and Locke reduced the body to its five senses—
the unhistorical open receptors of Newton's natural world.
Under these auspices the human eye and mind are merely mirrors of the empirical world. They are to see and dream no further. Nor is there any need. God's clockwork runs without him
and ours should do the same with proper education, for our
bodies and senses are like any other natural object. It is Blake,
of course, who challenges the Lockean philosophy of the five
senses in order to restore once again that imaginative body
which is the ground upon which we may resist equally natural-
ism and supernaturalism.[18] Blake struggles against the divisions
and natural anatomy of the vegetative body, against its shrink-
age and decay, against its fallen senses, sacrificed to sin, chast-
ity, and abhorrence, unsatisfied and self-destructive. The philosopher's body is a fallen body, natural and perspectival,
fragmented, yearning for wholeness through the radically passive domination of the world and ourselves to which we are
mostly mere witnesses. The *eye-culture* cripples self-conscious-
ness, observing it like a thing, *pars extra partes*, externalized, cast
out. The natural body binds itself to the real and the present,
above all to sexuality and property, contracting itself to a point,
turned away from the universe within the fourfold imaginative
body of Albion:

And every Man stood Fourfold. each Four Faces had. One to the
   West
One toward the East One to the South One to the North. the
   Horses
      Fourfold
And the dim Chaos brightened beneath, above, around! Eyed as
   the
      Peacock
According to the Human Nerves of Sensation, the Four Rivers of
   the
      Water of Life
South Stood the Nerves of the Eye. East in Rivers of bliss the
   Nerves

of the
Expansive Nostrils West, flowd the Parent Sense the Tongue.
North
    stood
The labyrinthine Ear. Circumscribing & Circumcising the
    excrementitious
Musk & Covering into Vacuum evaporating revealing the
    lineaments of
    Man
Driving outward the Body of Death in an Eternal Death &
    Resurrection
Awaking it to Life among the Flowers of Beulah reJoicing in
    Unity
In the Four Senses in the Outline the Circumference & Form, for
    ever
In Forgiveness of Sins which is Self Annihilation. It is the
    Covenant
        of Jehovah

[*Jerusalem*, 98, 12–23][19]

It is important not to reduce the autosymbolic work of the body to what Mircea Eliade calls "the world sexualized."[20] The anthropomorphization of the world is fashioned from all parts of the body. That is why I invoke the *gendered or familied body*, to be clear that I refer to a kinship of man, women and children, of past and future generations joined through a rich treasury of affiliation, place, and common sense. This is the first body of society—the wild body of all human culture. The gendered body is not the sexualized body. Otto Rank has argued persuasively that the anthropomorphic projection of the body represents a concern with wholeness and identity rather than with re-generation, which is a transition phase in creation: "Those theories which have made out that artistic creativity is the expression of the sexual impulse have only made use of a transition phase of man as creature to secularize the conception of man as creator. Indeed, this latter conception itself, as manifested in the idea of God, amounts to nothing less than an objectification of a creative urge that is no longer satisfied with self-reproduction, but must proceed to create an entire cosmos as the setting of that self."[21] Thus the liver, the navel, the head, the mouth, the upper vertebrae, the entrails, and the womb have all been symbolic sources in the search for microcosms of the universe. By a circuitous route from animal worship, from Babylon through Egypt and Greece into Christianity, there occurred a double shift—microcosmically, from the "lower-body" culture to the "upper-head" culture and, macrocosmically, from terrestial to celestial cultures. According to this pattern, the world breathes as a body breathes, each inhabited, as it were, by a material and a spiritual soul, or breath of life. The Greek *psyche* and the Latin *anima* both mean the breath-soul, the visible, tangible life that comes and goes, moving from the lower to the higher body until the intellect and reason become the seat of the soul. By the same token, the world becomes flesh, logos of the world, which is God.

Lévi-Strauss has pointed out that we cannot separate ourselves from so-called primitives on the ground that they lack the interest that we have in the objective classification of things, events, and relationships from which science is built.[22] The competence exhibited by the first human beings with respect to the categories of animals, vegetables, fruits, and minerals in their environment is proverbial. It is, moreover, an active, pragmatic competence and not merely a passive knowledge, confined to esoteric dictionaries. By the same token, these categorial systems exhibit an intrinsic preference for order over chaos; in this regard primitive thought is in a continuous line with science. Nor should we be deceived by the practice of the first humans of according the attributes of holiness, contamination, and taboo where science might speak only of "goodness of fit," or adequate generalization. There is little difference here. Things are holy inasmuch as they find their place, observe the norms of their kind, and do not contravene or threaten the orderliness in which people have an interest if their affairs are to prosper.

We must rather look upon primitive classifications as anticipations of modern science whose own strategy was to abstract from the sensory world in which early humans first found themselves and where, as Vico tells us, they were obliged to think with their sensory minds. The achievements of the first men and women in bringing forth pottery, weaving, metals, agriculture, the domestication of animals, as well as the rites of birth, marriage, and burial are enormous. It is impossible to conceive these elements of civilization as the result of anything else than a human preference for order and calculability concelebrated in the least resource involved in its production. Here I refer to the art, myth, and religion that recollect the creation of order. We therefore cannot ignore that neolithic people accumulated a long scientific tradition which still lies at the basis of modern natural science. Indeed, Lévi-Strauss argues that what is involved here are two complementary traditions of scientific inquiry differentiated according to the degree to which they are closer to or remote from "sensible intuition," or what with Vico I have called *sensory mind*:

> Myths and rites are far from being, as has often been held, the product of man's "myth-making faculty," turning its back upon reality. Their principal value is indeed to preserve until the present time the remains of methods of observation and reflection which were (and no doubt still are) precisely adapted to discoveries of a certain type: those which nature authorised from the starting point of a speculative organization and exploitation of the sensible world in sensible terms. This science of the concrete was necessarily restricted by its essence to results other than those destined to be achieved by the exact natural sciences but it was no less scientific and its results no less genuine. They were secured ten thousand years earlier and still remain at the basis of our own civilization.[23]

So far from being an early stage of thought, or one that might be allowed to atrophy with modern advances, those arts of sensible intuition Lévi-Strauss refers to under the notion of *bricolage* are what make scientific practice possible. The bricoleur is not tied to the distinctive materials or procedures of a given craft. Rather, he moves into a neighboring craft whenever the need to improvise arises, a need that he is able to see within the materials at hand although they are not explicitly designed for incorporation in his constructions. The bricoleur is an independent agent with respect to the conceptual and instrumental sets he has at hand, being capable of turning their built-in constraints to new combinations that surpass the limits of the old while respecting them. Mythical thinking and scientific thought both involve intellectual bricolage. And this common root is more significant than the outworn notion of the evolutionary distance between science and myth construction. Given any ready-made materials, the bricoleur may be said to create structures from events, or necessity from contingency, whereas the scientist creates events through the structures he imposes upon nature. In either case, artifacts intervene, whether as models or miniaturizations, in which the part/whole structures of the object are experimented with in a synthesis of natural and social events. And in terms of another analogy, science is like a game inasmuch as both create events through the imposition of a structure, whereas bricolage and myth resemble each other in treating historical and social events as indestructible pieces for recombined structures of the new and the same.

In this and the following chapters, then, I am urging us to think of the future shape of the world, nature, society, and the human family by recollecting our past creativity in self-shaping. In other words, I am saying that in order to make the future livable, we must not listen to those who seek to sever it from the past and to put the future, so to speak, in automatic gear. Our future is not something we can allow to be thrust upon us like some "new" detergent. The elitist visionaries of future technology reduce the human future to an element in our general culture of passive consumerism, to a promise of passive health and happiness. The ordinary person, who is each of us most of the time, needs to see that modern society and its future technologies of the mind, body, and political economy have not really come a long way without the enormous legacy of past human efforts. As ordinary people, therefore, we must insist upon the recollection of our cultural history through which we have brought ourselves to the frontier of modernism. We must insist upon our kinship with the world, with nature and wild life, and with the varied family cultures of the earth, realizing that there is far less distance between our past and the present than between today and a tomorrow without us.

It is this creed that I consider to be the deep structure of anthropomorphism. As such it is neither naive nor nostalgic. Of course, some might reach the opposite conclusion by seizing on the weakness and fallibility of human projection. From this standpoint, anthropomorphism is the last error of a nerveless humanism unable to live in a cosmos that refuses to mirror us. Here the paradox is that the currently fashionable antihumanism of social and literary systems without agents runs counter to the participatory epistemology of contemporary physics, which has abandoned the clockwork world of its early modern paradigm. Modern physics has restored the fundamental effects of embodied perception in its theory of knowledge. The complicity between the *embodied knower* and the objects of scientific knowledge requires that anthropomorphism be regarded as a constitutive feature of modern knowledge rather than as an idol of human ignorance.

Among those who have realized the implications of modern quantum physics, there is an urgent appeal for the renewal of holistic thinking.[24] Of course, this means flying in the face of all the liberal warnings about the errors and monstrosities of totalitarianism. But the real issue is one of whether we conserve or do not conserve the world's body, of *conservation*, and here the real enemy is neo-individualism as we have marketed it in North America and Western Europe (I do not mean to imply that the industrialized socialist economies are any the less dangerous to the human future of mankind). It is as easy as it is dangerous to beguile ourselves with the endless novelties of a future that will be produced without us. Everywhere we turn, there are proposals to redesign life, the mind, emotions, behavior, our work and living places in order to suit us to a high-tech future that will increasingly dispose of us, adding us to the world's already marginalized peoples whose diseased, famined, and homeless bodies never find peace and dignity on terms with the machine societies by whom they are dominated and discarded.

We have looked at the idea of an elaborate cosmography constructed upon the articulations and vital functions of man's communicative body. This conception of the world's body may seem remote to a society built upon the industrial conquest of nature. Yet whenever the excesses of this domination of nature are observed, as they are today, it becomes natural once again to remind ourselves of our kinship with the world's body—and thereby of our need to respect what is left of its wholeness. Radical anthropomorphism requires that we think the future shape of human beings according to a rule of conservation that places nature before life, yet life before society and the family before ourselves. To practice this rule, we must think the future as the present in order not to disconnect it from our everyday living and the fundamental ground of moral criticism which is rooted in our carnal knowledge of the good and evil we practice upon one another. It is in this sense, then, that the following chapters provide a backward look upon our future orientation.

CHAPTER TWO

SOCIAL BODIES

WHEN we turn from the world's body to look at the smaller world of human society, we are struck to find that people have also conceived the relation between their individual lives and the institutions of society in terms of the imagery of the human body. Lévi-Strauss observes: "The Australian tribes of the Drysdale River, in Northern Kimberley, divide all kinship relations, which together compose the social 'body,' into five categories named after a part of the body or a muscle. Since a stranger must not be questioned, he announces his kinship by moving the relevant muscle. In this case, too, therefore, the total system of social relations, itself bound up with a system of the universe, can be projected on to the anatomical plane."[1]

It is a conceit of ours that if society rules us at all it does so in our minds rather than in our bodies. We are, of course, enormously ambivalent about either side of these controls. We prefer to think that we rule our bodies rather than being ruled by them—without giving much thought to the body politic implicit in this conception of order (which we shall consider in the following chapter).[2] Likewise, we are aware of society's rule over us. But we prefer to think that society operates upon us intellectually and consensually rather than directly upon our bodies, which suggests a more slavish relation. In the final chapter we shall look at some specific issues in the exercise of modern *bio-power*, or the biotechnological redefinition of mind-body behavior basic to the therapeutic state. For the moment, however, I want to focus on the argument that social order in general is never just a cognitive construct or an abstract system of rules and categories to which individuals conform, whether freely or unfreely. I shall argue, instead, that there is an embodied logic of society or an embodied logic of social membership that furnishes the deep communicative structure of public life.

I propose, therefore, to set forth an explicitly Durkheimian conception of the interrelationship between our two bodies— the communicative and the physical. The basic feature of this approach to social organization is to treat its members' categorization of bodily attitudes, functions, and relations as socially learned and socially sanctioned embodiments of the "socio-logic" of public bodies. How such arguments proceed is nicely illustrated in Robert Hertz's study of the right hand.[3] So far as we can see, the resemblance between the right and left hands seem perfect. Yet, as we know, we use our hands quite differently, neglecting, avoiding, and even dishonoring the left hand, while preferring and according all sorts of privileges to the right. Each of us can imagine instances of the inequality we assign to our hands for particular purposes—as in greetings, or in wedding ceremonies. There are, of course, all sorts of variations in these practices. The whole matter may be dismissed as nothing but silly superstition or else quickly disposed of with a little knowledge of brain science. The latter settles the issue in the functional asymmetry of the brain, the dominance of the left side of the brain being responsible for the dominance of the right hand. In this case, as with so many other sociological phenomena, the competing accounts are themselves social phenomena. Curiously enough, the sneaking suspicion that we are dealing with superstition and not science is on the right track, despite its own deference toward science as the explanatory key. To put it from the other side, we may very well admit the basic phenomenon of organic asymmetry. Most people are righthanded, and relatively few are lefthanded—by nature, as we say—while others seem to be ambidexterous, educable to either side. Yet these facts are not sufficient to take account of the massive social preference for the right side over the left. In short, there is a pervasive dualist symbolism to which the right and left hand are assimilated as part of the world's order. Hertz writes: "How could man's body, the microcosm, escape the law of polarity which governs everything? Society and the whole universe have a side which is sacred, noble and precious, and another which is profane and common: a male side, strong and active, and another, female, weak and passive; or, in two words, a right and a left side—and yet the human organism alone should be symmetrical? A moment's reflection shows us that it is an impossibility. Such an exception would not only be an unexplicable anomaly, it would ruin the entire economy of the spiritual world."[4] In view of the amount of attention we have already given to the symbolism of the world's body, we can be more brief with its bearing upon the right hand. We can understand how it is that men will attribute strength and weakness, rectitude and turpitude, good fortune and evil to either side of their own bodies, as well as repeating this distribution between male and female bodies. Incidentally, the injustice in these attributions lies not in the impositions of one side upon the other; each is unthinkable without the other. Justice lies in the complementarity of the gendered parts; evil resides in the disturbance of the system. It is this economy which is respected in the Last Judgment, where the Lord's raised right hand points to the heavenly abode of the elect while his lowered left hand points the path toward the hell of the damned. Therefore, the right hand is raised in prayer, the right foot enters a holy place, and the wedding ring is taken in the right hand and placed upon the left finger; and the right hand takes oaths, gives blessings, stops the traffic. In all these cases, the right hand transmits the benign and blessed life-giving and life-preserving forces of the world's own right region. In view of this symbolism, the left side, the left hand, even the political left are thought to disturb justice and goodness wherever they seek to gain predominance over the right. And, if we seem fickle in giving turns to the right and left in dances, and in politics, might it not be that we still have deep respect for the balance of good and evil in our lives?

I shall argue, starting from this analogy, that *just as we think society with our bodies so, too, we think our bodies with society*. To do so I shall rely upon various studies by Mary Douglas,[5] both because they so nicely illustrate the bodily ties between individuals and institutions and because they help us to understand the relative claims of psychological and sociological analysis with respect to bodily conduct that it is otherwise tempting to consider wholly biopsychological in nature. Thus in all societies there are curiosities of behavior which center upon a concern with bodily dirt. Sometimes it is bodily parts, or bodily functions, or whole bodies, or classes of bodies that are considered sources of either purity or pollution. We generally keep ourselves clean but give ourselves an extra special wash and brush for special occasions—for dates, interviews, funerals, or our own weddings. We are as careful to avoid our own dirt, to remove it from sight, as we are to avoid the dirt of others. Moreover, with dirt, as with so many other matters related to the body, our concerns are not nearly so physical as moral. Mary Douglas notes:

> If we can abstract pathogenicity and hygiene from our notion of dirt, we are left with the old definition of dirt as matter out of place. This is a very suggestive approach. It implies two conditions: a set of ordered relations and a contravention of that order. Dirt, then, is never a unique, isolated event. Where there is dirt there is system. Dirt is the by-product of a systematic ordering and classification of matter, in so far as ordering involves rejecting inappropriate elements. This idea of dirt takes us straight into the field of symbolism and promises a link-up with more obviously symbolic systems of purity.[6]

Food in our mouths is where it should be; visible as we chew or on our chins it is disgusting. Sloppy eaters risk social and moral disapproval—the pain of being considered pigs or uncivilized. Here again, we see that the body is not just a biological entity. Eating, therefore, is not simply a matter of replacing the body's energy. To the extent that it is, eating approaches feeding—and McDonald's is a more appropriate setting for it than Maxime's. Human beings have to eat, to be sure. But to receive social and moral approval, they must eat like their own kind— like members of their own race, caste, class, religion, and age group. Not—when adults—like animals, savages, heathens, and babies.

In this regard, we may gain an insight into the otherwise curious provisions of the dietary rules and abominations of Leviticus, and, as I hope to show, of our own food culture:

> And the Lord spoke unto Moses and to Aaron, saying unto them,
>
> Speak unto the children of Israel, saying, These are the beasts which ye shall eat among all the beasts that are on earth.
>
> Whatsoever parteth the hoof, and is cloven-footed, and cheweth the cud among the beasts, that shall ye eat.
>
> Nevertheless these shall ye not eat of them that chew the cud, or of them that divide the hoof: the camel, because he cheweth the cud, but divideth not the hoof; he is unclean unto you.
>
> And the rock badger, because he cheweth the cud, but divideth not the hoof; he is unclean unto you.
>
> And the hare, because he cheweth the cud, but divideth not the hoof; he is unclean unto you.
>
> And the swine, though he divide the hoof, and be cloven-footed, yet he cheweth not the cud; he is unclean to you.
>
> Of their flesh shall ye not eat, and their carcass shall ye not touch; they are unclean to you.
>
> These shall ye eat of all that are in the waters: whatsoever hath fins and scales in the waters, in the seas, and in the rivers, them shall ye eat.
>
> And all that have not fins and scales in the seas, and in the rivers, of all that move in the waters, and of any living thing which is in the waters, they shall be an abomination unto you.
>
> They shall be even an abomination unto you; ye shall not eat of their flesh, but ye shall have their carcasses in abomination.
>
> Whatsoever hath no fins or scales in the waters, that shall be an abomination unto you.

And these are they which ye shall have in abomination among the fowls; they shall not be eaten, they are an abomination: the eagle, and the ossifrage, and the osprey,

And the kite, and falcon after its kind;

Every raven after its kind;

And the ostrich, and the night hawk, and the sea gull, and the hawk after its kind;

And the white owl, and the cormorant, and the horned owl,

And the swan, and the pelican, and the carrion eagle,

And the stork, and the heron after its kind, and the hoopoe, and the bat.

All winged insects, going upon all four, shall be an abomination unto you.

Yet these may ye eat of every winged insect that goeth upon all four, which have legs above their feet, with which to leap upon the earth;

Even these of them ye may eat: the locust after its kind, and the bald locust after its kind, and the beetle after its kind, and the grasshopper after its kind.

But all other winged insects, which have four feet, shall be an abomination unto you. . . .

And every creeping thing that creepeth upon the earth shall be an abomination; it shall not be eaten.

Whatsoever goeth upon the belly, and whatsoever goeth upon all four, or whatsoever hath many feet among all creeping things that creep upon the earth, them ye shall not eat; for they are an abomination.

Ye shall not make yourselves abomination with any creeping thing that creepeth, neither shall ye make yourselves unclean with them, that ye should be defiled thereby.

For I am the Lord your God: ye shall therefore sanctify your-selves, and ye shall be holy; for I am holy: neither shall ye defile yourselves with any manner of creeping that creepeth upon the earth.

For I am the Lord who bringeth you up out of the land of Egypt, to be your God; ye shall therefore be holy, for I am holy. [Lev. 11:1–23; 41–45]

The meaning of these rules has exercised biblical scholars for some time. By and large, either the rules are considered meaningless, serving only doctrinal purposes, or else they are thought to be allegories of virtues and vices. But in either case it is difficult to see what determines the general demarcation of clean from unclean animals, even though some cases fit practical rules of hygiene. Where allegorical interpretation is pursued, it amounts to little more than pious commentary—as when Philo finds those fish with fins and scales acceptable because they symbolize endurance and self-control, while those without are swept away by the current, without resisting or lifting themselves up by prayer! Some understanding may be possible, however, if we pay attention to the repeated injunction that accompanies the various exclusions in respect of animals, childbirth, leprosy, skin disease, and sexual secretions of the body—namely, the injunction to be *holy*: "For I am the LORD who bringeth you up out of the land of Egypt, to be your God; ye shall therefore be holy, for I am holy" (Lev. 11:45).

We must, then, look for the connections between holiness and the abominations. God's essential work is to create order through which men's affairs prosper—their women, livestock, and fields are kept fertile, their enemies, liars, cheats, and perverts destroyed or prevented. The holy man respects God's order and so enjoys his blessing. To infringe God's order is to run the risk of losing his blessing and suffering the consequences. Each thing in God's order must therefore respect its own kind and not risk hybridization, promiscuity, and perversion: "Thou shalt not lie with mankind, as with womankind: it is abomination. Neither shalt thou lie with any beast to defile thyself therewith; neither shall any woman stand before a beast to lie down thereto: it is confusion" (Lev. 18:22–23). Holiness, then, consists in preserving the classes of Genesis, and it is this injunction that is basic to the laws on clean and unclean meats. To preserve the convenant between Israel and God, the land, its cattle, and its people, the Israelites are enjoined from mixing, confusing, and disordering any of the categories of the earth, waters, and heavens. As Mary Douglas shows us (see Illustration 3), an order is revealed in the following schema:

(1) Animals are categorized according to their degree of holi-

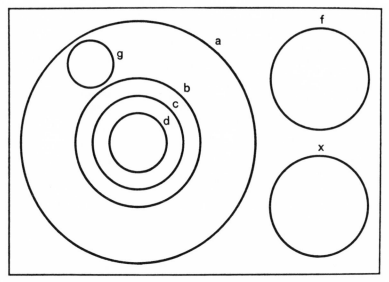

3. Denizens of the land (a) walk or hop with four legs; (b) fit for table; (c) domestic herds and flocks; (d) fit for altar; (f) abominable: insufficient criteria for (a); (g) abominable: insufficient criteria for (b); (x) abominable: swarming. Reproduced from Mary Douglas, "Deciphering a Meal," *Ecology in Theory and Practice*, ed. Jonathan Benthall, © The Institute of Contemporary Arts 1972, by permission of The Institute of Contemporary Arts.

ness, ranging from the abominable through those fit for the table, not the altar, to those fit for sacrifice. These degrees of holiness apply to all creatures, in the water, in the air, and on land.

(2) Only domesticated animals can be used as sacrificial offerings. Thus in the category of land creatures in the diagram (*a*), quadrupeds with parted hoofs and that chew the cud are fit for the table (*b*), and, from among these, domesticated herds and flocks (*c*) are the source for first-born offerings to the priest (*d*). The remaining categories represent anomalous creatures that live between two spheres or have hybrid morphological features; or else cut across all categories like the swarming, which are therefore the most abominable.

55

We can now trace how the rules enjoining the separation of animals function to sustain the separation of the Israelites from their neighbors. The common meal identifies the Jews both to themselves and to outsiders. It constitutes a political as well as a religious boundary between Jews and non-Jews. Can we say anything more specific about these prohibitions before we consider the rest of their syntactic relations? Jean Soler argues that the Mosaic laws must be related to the account of man's food given in Genesis:[7] "And God said, 'Behold, I have given you every herb bearing seed which is upon the face of all the earth, and every tree, in which is like fruit of a tree yielding seed; to you it shall be for food'" (Gen. 1:29).

In the first creation, paradise appears to be vegetarian. Adam is not to eat from the tree of knowledge, however. God preserves for himself immortality. He alone is the source of life. Man therefore may not take life. This difference between God and man is expressed in their respective foods. Only God may accept a living sacrifice. How then did men come to kill and eat meat? This is God's dispensation to Noah inasmuch as God saved his creation though he recognized its violence and murder. The third covenant, between God and Moses, separates the Hebrews from the rest of humankind; and it is here that we find the separations (cuts) of the Sabbath, circumcision, and the clean and unclean animals, which together constitute a symbolic system functioning to preserve Jewish religious and political identity. In particular, the taboo against blood is reinforced, so that the priest must make a peace offering of the blood of the sacrificial animal to appease God for the act of slaughter. In turn, the animals appropriate for the table and the altar are herbivorous rather than carnivorous, as though the animals themselves observed the injunction against slaughter, at least in the first Genesis account: "And to every beast of the earth, and to every foul of the air, and to everything that creepeth upon the earth, wherein there is life, I have given every green herb for food" (Gen. 1:30). Soler argues, therefore, that it is the "hoofed foot" which separates the herbivorous animals from the clawed predators on land and in the air. It remains to explain why clean animals have two further predicates, namely a "cloven hoof" and that they "chew the cud." The effect of the latter is to exclude pigs, which, though they have hoofed feet and are herbivorous, are also carnivorous. There remains some uncertainty about wild herbivorous animals, and therefore the "cloven hoof" is stressed, even though that rule eliminates from the category of clean animals such borderline cases of domestication as the camel, hare, horse, and ass, which are also herbivorous. Even so, clean domesticated animals must be perfect of their kind to be sacrificed. No animal—or person—with a blemish may participate in the holy sacrifice. By the same logic of wholeness, or of identity and holiness, nothing may be mixed in the kitchen or in bed that confuses the order of things. Soler writes:

> This no doubt explains the Bible's most mysterious prohibition: "You shall not boil a kid in its mother's milk" (Exod. 23:19 and 34:26; Deut. 14:21). These words must be taken quite literally. They concern a mother and her young. They can be translated as: you shall not put a mother and her son in the same pot, any more than into the same bed. Here as elsewhere, it is a matter of upholding the separation between two classes or two types of relationships. To abolish distinction by means of a sexual or culinary act is to subvert the order of the world. Everyone belongs to one species only, one people, one sex, one category. And in the same manner, everyone has only one God: "See now that I, even I, am he, and there is no God beside me" (Deut. 32:39). The keystone of this order is the principle of identity, instituted as the law of every being.[8]

Let us return to the analysis offered by Mary Douglas. We can see how the purity of the categories is metonymically reproduced in the purity of persons and animals. The Jews and their animals are separated and tied to one another through the rituals of purity in the same way that the Jews are separated from other people and their animals. Thus the first-born son and the first-born of the herds and flocks are equally consecrated to divine service: a mark that sets the people and its animals apart from other peoples and animals. As the first-born of the Israelites, the Levites are judges of their purity and among the Levites themselves only those without blemish may enter the Holy of Holies—the perfectly bounded sanctuary between God and man. The Jewish dietary rules, therefore, may be regarded as what Vico would call a "severe poem," dedicated to the political preservation of a people whose holiness is the mark of their will to survive.

Can we say more as to why the Jews (and Islamites) don't eat pork? There are in fact further questions to be settled with respect to the taxonomic status of the pig—as well as a wholly different approach to pigs as protein. Consider once again Leviticus 11:1–8. The pig is an unclean animal—like the hare, the hyrax, and the camel, it is an abomination. Because they do not have both cloven hoofs and the capacity to chew the cud, these animals are not clean. The pig, moreover, is the only land animal with cloven hoofs that does not chew the cud. Under pressure from critics,[9] Douglas came to see that, since anomalies may be either abominated or revered, animal taxonomies are best understood in relation to social rules about residence and marriage. Following Durkheim, we can expect the boundaries of natural classifications to be as permeable or impermeable as the boundaries of the social systems to which they belong.[10] Social boundaries are regulated by (among other things) the rules for marriage—the rules of exogamy and incest avoidance—whose effect is to admit strangers to the circle of kinsman. The Israelites had no prohibition against first-cousin marriages, which meant that in-marrying was preferred to marriage alliances either with other lineages or tribes among the Israelites or with foreigners. Surrounded by enemies, the Jews were particularly vexed by the problem of the stranger, especially since some, like the Samaritans, also claimed to be Israelites. The Jews could marry prisoners of war, and obviously they had absorbed the Canaanites. The risk taken in marrying strangers entailed the risk of eating their food, and the pig was more likely to be sacrificed for a wedding than the camel or hare. Therefore in the same way that the Jews insisted upon their historical identity, they also insisted upon the identity of Jahweh and of their own classes of clean and unclean animals. Douglas concludes: "It would seem that whenever a people are aware of encroachment and danger, dietary rules controlling what goes into the body would serve as a vivid analogy of the corpus of their cultural categories at risk."[11]

Here, then, we have a fine example of the socio-logic of incorporation that underlies the concept of the body politic, to the general history of which we shall turn in the next chapter. Before doing so, however, we should consider a more directly materialist challenge to Douglas's political account of pig taxonomy and political history. Among a number of essays directly or indirectly responding to Douglas that have raised quite a storm are Marvin Harris's speculations on the love/hatred of the pig prevalent among Jews and Moslems, excluding them from the succulence of roast pig celebrated in Lamb's essay, as well as depriving them from an extremely efficient protein processor:[12]

> The pig taboo recurs throughout the entire vast zone of Old World pastoral nomadism—from North Africa across the Middle East and Central Asia. But in China, South East Asia, Indonesia and Melanesia the pig was and still is a much-used source of dietary proteins and fats, as it is in modern Europe and the Western Hemisphere. The fact that the pig was tabooed in the great pastoral zones of the Old World and in several of the river valleys bordering these zones suggests that the Biblical taboos must be seen as an adaptive response valuable over a wide area in relation to recurrent ecological shifts brought about by the intensification and depletions associated with the rise of ancient states and empires.[13]

Harris argues that with the rise of the ancient states, and the larger populations they required, it was necessary to shift from raising pigs, sheep, goats, and cattle primarily for meat and to put more land under the plough for wheat, barley, and other plant crops, which have roughly ten times greater calorie return than the animal sources gained by the same expenditure. In short, Harris claims, there was a decision to raise and feed people on plant crops rather than raise and feed meat-pro-

59

ducing animals for a smaller return. In addition, the use of domesticated animals changed; instead of being a meat source of
proteins, they became a milk-based protein source. While this
particular strategy may have been rational, Harris claims that
with respect to the consumption of basic amino acids, the shift
from meat to plant foods resulted in a diminishing standard of
nutrition, health, and vigor. Furthermore, he claims that because the pig has no use other than meat-protein production,
even though it yields two or three times as many calories as
cattle or chickens, it was the first domestic species to become
too expensive to raise and thus to incur religious taboo. This
change in the nutritional status of the pig resulted in large part
from a shift in the ratio of grassland to forest, where the pig
finds the kind of tubers, roots, fruits, and nuts it most efficiently
converts to meat. Above all, it finds in the forest the shade it
needs, since pigs, Harris says, cannot regulate their body tem-
perature by sweating (actually, pigs sweat like pigs by wallow-
ing).[14] When the Israelites arrived in Palestine, they rapidly con-
verted the forests in the Judaean and Samaritan hills to pasture
land. Consequently, pig raising became much more expensive,
however tempting. Hence the taboos upon the pig as an unclean animal reinforced the need to avoid its domestication in
large numbers that would have to be fed on grain supplements
that could more efficiently be used for human consumption.

Harris is aware that there is a certain redundancy in this materialist account. If humans are by nature economists, why in
the face of the inefficiency of pig production would they be
tempted to raise pigs? Why would the poor Irish need meatless
Fridays when they could easily see that fish was a cheaper
source of protein?[15] He nevertheless argues that the cost/benefit
principle applied equally well to the rest of the unclean animals
insofar as they were both in short supply and obtainable only
by hunting. Since pastoralists were not likely to be good at
hunting or fishing and would get little meat from such efforts,
the religious taboos contained in Leviticus prove that its authors
were able economists rather than poor doctors or classificatory
maniacs. Rather than treating the pig taboo in terms of pecu-

liarly Israelite concerns with taxonomy and religious identity, Harris concludes that it, and similar curiosities, can be understood only as an economic response to a shifting food environment: "The link between the depletion of animal proteins on the one hand, and the practice of human sacrifice and cannibalism, the evolution of ecclesiastical redistributive feasting, and the tabooing of the flesh of certain animals on the other, demonstrates the unmistakable causal priority of material costs and benefits over spiritual beliefs—not necessarily for all time, but almost certainly for the cases in question."[16]

I cannot close off this controversy without bringing it into the orbit of the structuralist approach to the categorization of human beings, animals, and food. I do so in only the simplest fashion and more with a view to providing Harris's opponent, Marshall Sahlins, with a voice than to entering into the labyrinths of Lévi-Strauss's thought.[17] It is tempting to see in Harris's thesis a strong version of the materialist arguments that might characterize a Marxist anthropology. Yet it is in the name of a Marxist cultural anthropology that Sahlins rejects Harris's reduction of practical reason to the sheerest calculation. We are concerned with people's relation to their food. It might be thought that such a relation is sheerly bioeconomic. Humans need a diet that will more than replace the energy they expend in procuring it. That is the sole significance of food and eating. Yet people seem to distinguish themselves from animals in that we eat whereas animals feed. In view of the largely learned and socially organized classification of foods considered edible and inedible, together with elaborate codes for their preparation and serving, it seems unlikely that Harris's cost benefit theorem can be the complete explanation. Indeed, utilitarianism of any sort is generally a poor guide to what it is consumers pursue in making their lives longer and, more beautiful, sexy, and self-assured. Utilitarianism or materialism is rather the form of consciousness through which bourgeois society hides from itself its nonrational economy, as we shall see in Chapter 4.

The symbolic values that circulate in both the production and the consumption sectors of the economy cannot be reduced to a pragmatic logic of efficiency except at the cost of hiding from ourselves the larger cultural economy in which we labor and consume. To show the truth of this proposition, Sahlins offers his own account[18] of the cultural preferences underlying American food habits, drawing upon work of Douglas, Edmund Leach and Lévi-Strauss that we have already considered in its bare essentials. Thus meat is the center of the American meal. Steak in particular is a man's food. It is American, recalling the hard work of ranching, the sagas of cowboys and Indians, and a way of life for men halfway between the nomad and the townsman. Americans eat meat. They eat steaks, hamburgers, pork, and ham; but they do not eat horses and dogs. Unlike the French, they do not to any extent even feed horses to dogs. Rather, they go to elaborate lengths to feed dogs and cats like themselves, though perhaps assigning to their pets more entrails or offal than their owners care for. How are we to explain such curiosities? Once again, we can entertain rival explanations. Americans, it will be said, are the world's busiest people. They therefore collectively use and produce enormous quantities of energy ranging from hydroelectricity to oil and, of course, proteins on the individual level. The American body is an energy factory, producing health, strength, youth, smiles, sex, and satisfaction. Naturally, the American diet is geared to all this. Not withstanding the malnutritional aspects of fast food chains, *fast food is the essential American food*. In other words, Americans eat high on the hog; and when they stop to look around, they view those who don't as either poor, unsuccessful, lazy, or sick, or else as food freaks opting out of the mainstream, munching on vegetarian diets and nonaggressive philosophies of life. Meat, the mainstay of the American way of life, is identical with American strength and industriousness.

Following Leach, let us look at how the domesticated animal series—cattle, pigs, horses, dogs, regarded as a chain of decreasing edibility—might be mapped against a series of social relations representing decreasing degrees of community/commensality.[19] Thus it is noticeable that there are fairly strong distinctions between edible and inedible animals, and similarly within the edible category—cattle and pork—a strong distinction between the "meat" and the "innards" of the animals. In other words, Americans observe a food taboo with respect to horses and dogs and are squeamish, at least, about innards. Why do they think their food this way? In accordance with Leach's argument, we may notice that the food taboo correlates with the kinship series insofar as horses and dogs share human company, have names, are friends, and can be loved. Cattle and pigs are less human in this respect. Eating the meat of these animals is eating less of the quintessential animal than eating its innards, again preserving the boundary between humans and animals despite the daily necessity of infringing it. This boundary is in turn reproduced socioeconomically in that the higher classes can afford more steak than the lower; the poorer, especially blacks, being driven to "cheaper cuts" and, of course, to innards.

Can we radically rethink society with our bodies? Or are we caught in categorical systems that think us? To conclude, I would like to take a second look at the symbolic status of meat in the American economy. It is generally thought that Americans are among the best fed people in the world. It is part of this conventional wisdom that American charity is typically disbursed in the form of food and grain to starving people elsewhere. Actually, American dairy dumping and the protein myth have considerable transnational effects upon weaker agricultural societies.[20] In reality, the United States is no more self-sufficient in food than in any other enterprise on which the American economy prides itself. The terrible truth is that the United States shares in the Western world's net importation of proteins from the undernourished (and frequently starving) Third World. The geographer and food scientist Georg Borgstrom writes: "Through oil seeds (peanuts, palm kernels, copra, etc.), oilseed products, and fish meal, the Western world is currently acquiring from the hungry world one million metric tons more protein than is delivered to the hungry world through grains. In other words, the Western world is exchanging approximately 3 million metric tons of cereal protein for 4 million

63

metric tons of other proteins which are all superior in nutritive aspects."[21]

What is even more astonishing is the nature of the production process that supplies the American passion for meat as a central dish, whether at home, in restaurants, or in fast food chains. The cycle begins with the enormously increased productivity of American grains as a result of genetic seed improvements and the use of fertilizers and pesticides. We ignore the health hazards resulting from these procedures, though they bear, of course, on the issues to be considered in the later chapter on medical bodies. Americans ingeniously give grain away, waste food, and dump dairy products abroad, but nothing disposes of as much American grain as the American steer. In the conversion of plant protein to animal protein, the average steer requires sixteen pounds of grain per pound of meat on the table, hogs require six, turkeys four, chickens three, and milk one per pint. Or, to look at the matter the other way around, an acre of cereals yields five times more protein than an acre given to meat production; an acre of beans, peas, or lentils is ten times more efficient, and leafy vegetables fifteen times in producing protein. The American steer is a protein factory in reverse!

Furthermore, to keep meat enshrined in the American food market it is necessary to maintain the feedlot operation—the forced feeding of grains, soybeans, milk products, fish meal, wheat germ under assembly line conditions that also require the introduction of hormones and antibiotics—with incidental health risks to American consumers and the certain risk of starvation to millions elsewhere in the world. The author of *Diet for a Small Planet* notes:

If we exclude dairy cows, the average conversion ratio for U.S. livestock is 7 pounds of grain and soy feed to produce one pound of edible meat. (Note that this figure is an *average* of relatively high [chicken] and low [steer] efficiency converters.) According to this estimate, of the 140 million tons of grain and soy we fed to our beef cattle, poultry and hogs in 1971, *one-seventh*, or only 20 million tons, was returned to us in meat. *The rest, almost 118 million tons of grain and soy, became unaccessible for human consumption.* Although we lead the world in exports of grain and soy, this incredible volume "lost" through livestock was twice the level of our current exports. It is enough to provide every single human being on earth with more than a cup of cooked grain each day of the year![22]

We are, then, what we do or do not eat; and the same may be said of society. Our bodies are social in almost any way we care to think, and yet it is our bodies we claim from society as our most intimate and private possession. In a world where multitudes starve and others suffer from obesity, still others pin to themselves "edibaubles," rings, pins, necklaces, and earrings of plastic junk-food shapes, hamburgers, hot dogs, and apple pie. Meantime, cookbooks and gourmet food guides continue to proliferate what has been called "gastro-porn,"[23] whisking the urban aesthete into pastorales of fresh fruit and vegetables, blending New York and Provence, mixing morals and madness, economy and extravagance, all in a world of vicarious sensations whose only rival appears to be that of the sex manuals, whose metaphors are equally gastronomic. It might be added that both are solipsistic arts, idylls of selfish reconciliation to the decline of the embodied family.

In this chapter, then, I have tried to show how two social orders, each meat-minded, nevertheless connect to different orders of political economy and religion. In the case of biblical Judaism, religion and politics confirm the will to survive celebrated in a holy meal. In North America, the totemic meal confirms industriousness celebrated in ever faster foods. I have argued that we should rethink our meat culture in the light of the world's food economy. We must also foster a critical intelligence about our health habits in respect of the rest of our food as it passes from the farm, through the factory, store, home, and restaurant. By now there is a great deal of concern over the health hazards manufactured into our food. Everyone must be made aware of this. Our families and schools as well as the media must educate children, youth, and new families in these issues.

65

The task cannot be left to the goodwill of the food corporations geared to the "family" in the fast lane. We must insist, then, that *the family should be a thinking body*, whose common sense should be fostered in any healthy community and by any practical means. As this book proceeds, I shall formulate further propositions aimed at interceding on behalf of the critical function of a familied intelligence.

CHAPTER THREE

THE BODY POLITIC

EVERY political community has to find a symbolic expression of its beliefs concerning the sources, sustenance and potential threats to the orderly conduct of its members. Thus the imagery of the *body politic* recurs in our reflections on the nature of order and disorder in the human community. From the plebeian secession from Rome to the street politics of the sixties and today's antinuclear war protests, the human body has provided the language and the very text of political protest against and confrontation with the agencies that administer our inhumanity. This rhetorical conception of the body politic for which I shall argue differs from rhetoric concerned with an administrative science of politics in that it can be developed to enhance *the communicative competence of citizen democracy* to a significant extent. Hitherto the logic of calculative rationality has dominated the production and maintenance of social order, making alternative conceptions of society seem utopian and irrational. However, the repressive functions of administrative rationality have inevitably led its critics to a search for a new political symbolism, a search whose reasonableness may be conveyed through an analysis of the classical concept of the body politic. The body politic is the fundamental structure of our political life. It provides the grounds of ultimate appeal in

67

times of deep institutional crisis, of hunger and alienation, when there is need to renew the primary bonds of political authority and social consensus. Our appeal to the logic of the body seeks to re-embed the now hegemonic technological and bureaucratic knowledge in the common-sense *bioknowledge* of persons and families whose lives are otherwise administered by the modern corporate economy and its therapeutic state. The urgency of this issue will be seen in Chapter 5 when we consider the technologies of medicalized power that characterize the therapeutic state.

Leonard Barkan has suggested that we can trace roughly three stages in the development of the anthropomorphic image of the universe and society:

(1) *simple anthropomorphism*: This is the stage we have called the world's body. As Vico pointed out, early humans had nothing else but their bodies with which to think the cosmos and society;

(2) *the organic cosmos*: In this stage the body imagery in thinking the universe and society has become abstract, its puzzles are explored. Here important elements of ancient and medieval philosophical, cosmological and theo-political thought are bequeathed to us, as we shall see further in this chapter, which also explores the next stage:

(3) *the renewal of the body politic*: From time to time the imagery of the human body is again made sharp to reassert the human shape of human beings where they are threatened by social and political forces directed at administering men and women as things or automata.[1] Here, then, we may speak of radical anthropomorphism, and I shall develop this insight in an effort to rethink the body politic in response to the dilemmas of everyday life in the modern administrative state with its therapeutic apparatus.

We shall first review the legacy of classical and medieval thought on the body politic. Plato could approach the nature of the *polis* only by looking for the integrative principle that made it more than a physical or natural collection.[2] Thus, while the

68

human body places men and women in a natural collection, it is nevertheless true that social and political life brings them together in virtue of some principle higher than natural necessity, inasmuch as men and women are also rational and moral animals. Thus the true polis arises out of a "first city" that is, as it were, merely *the body writ large*. The first city is constituted in terms of a system of exchange in wants and needs which unites men and women collectively, just as the various needs of their bodies drive them to maintain their individual bioconstitutions. In this first city, health and harmony are achieved through the coordination of the arts of trade and commerce, just as the health of the body consists in the satisfaction of its various members. It turns out, however, that the first city becomes feverish in the search for luxuries, engages in war, and consequently needs to be reorganized through the inclusion of a class of guardians, whose proper education further requires a class of philosophers with insight into the true health of the polis. Although the true health of the body is nothing more than what it was before it became sick, the art of its restoration has no counterpart in nature. The work of the physician and, by analogy, the work of the political philosopher is the work of reason. Insight into the true object of that work may be gained by treating the polis as a soul writ large, though I am unable to pursue this line any further.

Perhaps the most famous account of the revolutionary body politic is that given by Menenius Agrippa in his effort to avoid the plebeian secession at a critical stage in Rome's history:

> Long ago when the members of the human body did not, as now they do, agree together, but had each its own thoughts and the words to express them in, the other parts resented the fact that they should have the worry and trouble of providing everything for the belly, which remained idle, surrounded by its ministers, with nothing to do but enjoy the pleasant things they gave it. So the discontented members plotted together that the hand should carry no food to the mouth, that the mouth should take nothing that was offered it, and that the teeth should accept nothing to chew. But alas! while they sought in their resentment to subdue

the belly by starvation, they themselves and the whole body wasted away to nothing. By this it was apparent that the belly, too, has no mean service to perform: it receives food, indeed; but it also nourishes in its turn the other members, giving back to all parts of the body, through all its veins, the blood it has made by the process of digestion; and upon this blood our life and our health depend.[3]

We know, of course, that the imagery of the body politic continued to be exploited throughout the ancient and medieval period. Aristotle, Cicero, Seneca, and numerous other writers drawing upon them repeated the tropes of harmony, balance, fever, and disproportion as principal figures of political thought. A major elaboration upon these figures occurs in Saint Paul's doctrine of the *mystical body* in which the unity in difference that sustains the members of the human body is appealed to as the basis for the charismatic unity of the members of a Christian society, where each exercises his talents on behalf of the others, and always as a gift of God rather than as his own property. The sublimity of the Christian conception of unity in difference is marvelously contained in the circular figures of Christ's body (Illustration 4), which simultaneously contains the tree of life, abstracting and protecting the intimacy of its members. Here, through these two intimate figures, the circle and the tree, we enter the boundless space of God, yet proportioned to the incarnate Christ-Man. Saint Paul depicted the image as follows:

> Now there are diversities of gifts, but the same Spirit.
> And there are differences of administrations, but the same Lord.
> And there are diversities of operations, but it is the same God who worketh all in all.
> But the manifestation of the Spirit is given to every man to profit. . . .
> For as the body is one, and hath many members, and all the members of that one body, being many, are one body, so also is Christ.

For by one Spirit were we all baptized into one body, whether we be Jews or Greeks, whether we be bond or free; and have been all made to drink into one Spirit.

For the body is not one member, but many.

If the foot shall say, Because I am not the hand, I am not of the body; is it, therefore, not of the body?

And if the ear shall say, Because I am not the eye, I am not of the body; is it, therefore, not of the body?

If the whole body were an eye, where were the hearing? If the whole were hearing, where were the smelling?

But now hath God set the members, every one of them, in the body, as it hath pleased him.

And if they were all one member, where were the body?

But now are they many members, yet but one body.

And the eye cannot say unto the hand, I have no need of thee; nor again the head to the feet, I have no need of you.

Nay, much more those members of the body which seem to be more feeble, are necessary:

And those members of the body, which we think to be less honorable, upon these we bestow more abundant honor; and our uncomely parts have more abundant comeliness.

For our comely parts have no need, but God hath tempered the body together, having given more abundant honor to that part which lacked,

That there should be no schism in the body, but that the members should have the same care one for another.

And whether one member suffer, all the members suffer with it; or one member be honored, all the members rejoice with it. [1 Cor. 12:4–26][4]

One of the most remarkable developments in the imagery of the body politic occurred in the fusion of certain doctrines of high medieval political theology with the legal fiction of the King's Two Bodies—the *body natural* and the *body politic*:

The King has two Capacities, for he has two Bodies, the one whereof is a Body natural, consisting of natural Members as every other Man has, and in this he is subject to Passions and Death as other Men are; the other is a Body politic, and the Members

4. Manuscript illumination, Christ, c. 1341. Reproduced with the permission of the publisher from Alžběta Güntherová and Ján Mišianik, *Illuminierte Handschriften aus der Slowakei* (Prague: Artia).

thereof are his Subjects, and he and his Subjects together compose the Corporation, as Southcote said, and he is incorporated with them, and they with him, and he is the Head, and they are the members, and he has the sole Government of them; and this Body is not subject to Passions as the other is, nor to Death, for as to this Body the King never dies, and his natural Death is not called in our Law (as Harper said), the Death of the King, but the Demise of the King, not signifying by the Word (Demise) that the Body politic of the King is dead, but that there is a Separation of the two Bodies, and that the Body politic is transferred and conveyed over from the Body natural now dead, or now removed from the Dignity royal, to another Body natural. So that it Signifies a Removal of the Body politic of the King of this Realm from one Body natural to another.[5]

The fiction of the king's two bodies, as is evident from a closer look at the wording of the preceding passage, draws upon the corporate doctrine of the Roman church elaborated in Carolingian times from sources in Saint Paul. Roughly, what happened is that the mystical body of Christ (the Eucharist) and the body of Christ (the church and the faithful on earth throughout history) merged in response to controversy over the real presence of Christ in the Eucharist. Thus the Eucharist became simply *corpus christi* (formerly Christian society) and the church became *corpus mysticum*, formerly the term for the Eucharist. So at the very time when the church was beginning to achieve recognition as a secular power among other secular legal and political institutions, it thereby offered to these institutions the distinction between Christ's natural body and his spiritual or ecclesiastical body. Ernst Kantorowicz writes:

> it had been the custom to talk about the Church as the "mystical body of Christ" (*corpus Christi mysticum*) which sacramentally alone makes sense. Now, however, the Church, which had been the mystical body of Christ, became a mystical body in its own right. That is, the Church organism became a "mystical body" in an almost juristic sense: a mystical corporation. The change in terminology was not haphazardly introduced. It signified just another step in the direction of allowing the clerical corporational

73

institution of the *corpus ecclesiae iuridicum* to coincide with the *corpus ecclesiae mysticum* and thereby to "secularize" the notion of "mystical body."[6]

Moreover, this shift in terminology made it easier for the pope to be the political head of the church's secular body politic than of the Eucharistic body of the church. By the same token, the terminology was in place for the juridical appropriation by the strictly secular body politic of the spiritual and transcendental predicates of the mystical body. It remained for the jurists to work out the doctrines of the corporate continuity of the state. In particular, there was the problem of furnishing the king with two bodies so that his natural "demise" could be survived by his body politic. We cannot follow the arguments whereby further distinctions were elaborated concerning the public and private capacities of the king, the inalienable sovereignty of the people, and the relative claims of natural and positive law. What I want to stress is that medieval corporate theory was never tempted to the later-nineteenth-century fictions of the organic or totalitarian state. The medieval tradition, on the contrary, split the two sovereignties of the state and the individual. This tradition, certain features of which I argue below for reviving, has always resisted any fiction of the state as a higher spiritual entity.

During the Renaissance, political thinkers continued to employ body imagery as a guide to thinking the relation between the head of the state and its members.[7] Thus it was conceivable to Aeneas Sylvius when he wrote his *De ortu et auctoritate imperie romani* (1466), a treatise on the origins and authority of Roman rule, that the prince's head might be sacrificed like a hand or a foot, if it saved the life of the body politic. It was axiomatic to this way of thinking that the body had a prior claim to life over its members: herein lay also the possibility of defending lies, deception, and injustice toward individuals if it served the corporate body. Of course, Aeneas Sylvius (later Pope Pius II) could hardly have envisaged anything salutary in a decapitated state. Yet for later regicides this issue might have been more difficult without the doctrine of the king's two bodies, the one secular and disposable, the other spiritual and hence not biodegradable. How the body image functioned with respect to the possibility of an acephalous state is nicely portrayed in Sir John Fortescue's defense of a moderate monarchy written in the years from 1468 to 1471:

> Saint Augustine, in the 19th book of the *De Civitate Dei*, chapter 23, said that a *A people is a body of men united by consent of law and by community of interest*. But such a people does not deserve to be called a body whilst it is acephalous, i.e. without a head. Because, just as in natural bodies, what is left over after decapitation is not a body, but is what we call a trunk, so in bodies politic a community without a head is not by any means a body. Hence Aristotle in the first book of the *Politics* said that *Whensoever one body is constituted out of many, one will rule, and the others be ruled*. So a people wishing to erect itself into a kingdom or any other body politic must always set up one man for the government of all that body, who, by analogy with a kingdom, is, from *"regendo"*, usually called a king. As in this way the physical body grows out of the embryo, regulated by one head, so the kingdom issues from the people, and exists as a body mystical, governed by one man as head. And just as in the body natural, as Aristotle said, the heart is the source of life, having in itself the blood which it transmits to all the members thereof, whereby they are quickened and live, so in the body politic the will of the people is the source of life, having in it the blood, namely, political forethought for the interest of the people, which it transmits to the head and all the members of the body, by which the body is maintained and quickened.[8]

Thus between Aeneas Sylvius and Sir John Fortescue we see an interesting alternation. If the prestige of the head over the heart and stomach is preserved, the body politic leans toward authority; whereas if the vital services of the stomach or the heart are emphasized, it leans toward moderate monarchy. (It would be wrong to speak of democracy in the latter case, since no one favored a body with many heads!) To vary the image just slightly, the prince as the physician of the body politic may be considered the source of the troubles from which his patients suffer and more likely to heal them by forebearing the exercise of his crude medicine. Such was the opinion of Montaigne, whose skepticism with regard to medicine was even greater than it was toward philosophy: "The preservation of states is a thing that probably surpasses our understanding. As Plato says, a civil government is a powerful thing and hard to dissolve. It often holds out against mortal internal disease, against the mischief of unjust laws, against tyranny, against the excesses and ignorance of the magistrates and the licence and sedition of the people."[9] However, where the prince is seen as a philosophical doctor, as by Budé or Erasmus, then we have a more trusting view of his ministrations than otherwise seems justified by princely ignorance and corruption. In either case, the body politic does well to be sturdy, evenly balanced and not subject to extremes of temperament and wealth if it is to survive the ministrations of its rulers. Thus, Machiavelli also based his rude political advice upon the capacity of the "mixed" body to survive change and destruction and to renew itself.[10] Generally, however, the body image served the interests of limited monarchy, as well expressed once again by Sir John Fortescue:

The law, indeed, by which a group of men is made into a people, resembles the nerves of the body physical, for, just as the body is held together by the nerves, so this body mystical is bound together and united into one by the law, which is derived from the word "ligando", and the members and bones of this body, which signify the solid basis of truth by which the community is sustained, preserve their rights through the law, as the body natural does through the nerves. And just as the head of the body physical is unable to change its nerves, or to deny its members proper strength and due nourishment of blood, so a king who is head of the body politic is unable to change the laws of that body, or to deprive that same people of their own substance uninvited or against their wills. You have here, prince, the form of the institution of the political kingdom, whence you can estimate the power that the king can exercise in respect of the law and the subjects, and their bodies and goods, and he has power to this end issuing from the people, so that it is not permissible for him to rule his people with any other power.[11]

With these passages in mind, I hope to avoid any suggestion that in the following attempt to revive certain features of the ancient and medieval conception of the body politic[12] I am reversing the liberal individualist tradition in favor of an organicist and totalitarian conception of political life. Rather, as I see it, it is precisely because the modern liberal administrative state has succumbed to "organization" that we find ourselves trying to rethink the body politic. Admittedly, in the face of the modern administrative state and its concomitant civic privatism, trying to revive the imagery of the body politic is a huge challenge to the political imagination. The weight of political rhetoric is all in the other direction. That is to say, political discourse is increasingly shaped to the legitimation needs of the administrative state and its agenda for public and private allocations of socioeconomic goods and services.[13] To make possible the state's intervention in major domains of social and economic life, it is necessary to treat the administration of these areas as the task of expert technical sciences, whose professional practice requires a client- or patient-model of citizenry. Thus, as Jürgen Habermas has argued, we find that the administrative state requires the depoliticization of the public realm, and brings that about by fostering simultaneously (1) *civic privatism*: the pursuit of consumption, leisure, and careers in exchange for political abstinence; (2) *public depoliticization*: the ideological justification of (1) by means of elitist theories of the democratic process and by technocratic accounting procedures that rationalize administrative power.[14] These two strategies encourage a species of familism divorced from any critical and public intelligence. This process is compounded by the dependency of the liberal welfare state upon the multinational corporate agenda and, indeed, the welfare state is obliged much of the time to sustain the fiction of political sovereignty in a shadow fight with an agile opponent who is not even in the same ring. Furthermore, the multinational corporations can presume an *ex post facto* ratification of their allocation of resources between private and public goods and services inasmuch as the state underwrites the gap between the promise and the actual performance of the market by means of its own economic activities, even while it is claiming that these restore a rational social agenda. These strategies require a technical style of political discourse to which the imagery of the body politic is foreign.

Yet the fact is that men and women, and especially many young people, are unhappy with the administration of their lives. They perceive this dissatisfaction not simply as resulting from economic exploitation but also as a state of pervasive *linguistic alienation* from the bureaucratic and administrative discourse of the experts who function on behalf of the state, schools, hospitals, and social agencies. The rationalization of the administered society requires that political discourse be problem-specific and subject to decisionistic or calculative reasoning. In turn, the very scientificity of the language and reportage of the social sciences contributes to the administrative effort to manage behavior and institutions according to standards of maximum efficiency. The latter, however, are ill suited for dealing with the daily experience of unemployment, ignorance, and teen-age suicide and pregnancies which falls upon families, churches, and local agencies that must cope as best they can. Moreover, the administered society's ability by and large to command allegiance in exchange for granting participation in goods and services reduces political participation to the demand for "information" about irreversible events, disapproval of which we have a residual right to express in elections. The combined effect of these processes upon the communicative competence of citizens, families, churches, and local communities is that discourse about the ideal values of political, economic, and social life is marginalized and alienated as talk lacking any rational—that is, decisionistic—grammar.

Elsewhere, I have tried to show that street antics, rock music, and the dirty-speech movement, for example, despite their apparently irrational and destructive appearance, represented real expressions of the communicative competence of populations responding to corporate and military domination. At first sight, from the participants' speech, dress, and improvised resources, these movements appeared to be impoverished attempts to confront the legitimacy of the corporate, economic, and political system. In actual fact, they exhibited a highly literate and artistic rationality as adult subversion of the processes of mass loyalty and civic privacy. Their very transgression of the boundaries of public and private language testified to the arbitrariness of the vested interests in the symbiosis between political information and public silence. Behind the antics of the sixties lay an articulate expression of the right to participate in the intellectual, linguistic, and artistic resources of the body politic, whose members otherwise sicken in silence and obedience. Moreover, these demands came from middle-class, literate students whose very production, in terms of the proliferation of universities and the rationalizations of the educational process, was designed to recruit them to the tasks of the administered economy. These are the people who played with gender, dress, work, and authority, who challenged the conventions of adult and child relationships and questioned the separation between art and politics. They were also peculiarly the benefactors and the victims of the role of the media in modern politics. As benefactors, they got the coverage and display that fueled the international spread of the student movement. They were victims in that their bodily antics, clashes, and confrontations served the media in the conveyance of the palpable disorder and implied irrationality of their demands.

A considerable ideological effort has been made both in the media and academia to erase the sixties from our political memory. Yet, more than ever, people continue to look for reasonable articulations of the body politic in order to express their concern with environmental pollution, genocide, family breakdown, threats to the bodily integrity of women and children, unwholesome food, inadequate medicine, and the like, since these are the issues where political welfare becomes intelligible and valuable to them. Families and individuals want to know what institutions and powers shape their physical and mental health, what determines their conditions of work and their standard of living, as well as what influences the chances of war and peace. From the standpoint of these fundamental concerns, I believe we need to replace the dominant imagery of administrative and organizational science with a three-level model of the body politic:

Levels	Institutions	Discourse
the bio-body	family	well-being, health, sickness
the productive body	work	self-control, exploitation
the libidinal body	personality	happiness, creativity, discontent

The *bio-body politic* represents a way of collecting the interest men and women have in their well-being, bodily health, and reproduction. The welfare of the family is iconic of the satisfaction of these demands. The *productive body politic* represents a complex organization of labor and intellect expended in the material and social reproduction of life. Here we speak of an active and creative worker. The *libidinal body politic* represents a level of desire that fulfills the order of personality insofar as it transcends the goods of family and economy and aspires to that highest unreachable intelligence, to love and happiness.

So long as men and women continue to be birthed and familied of one another, the bodily, social, and libidinal orders of living will not be separable worlds. By the same token, the body politic cannot be reduced to purely economistic satisfactions any more than to the dream of love's body. It is a distinctive feature of the metaphor of the body politic that it allows us to stand away from *mechano-morphism*, that is, machine, cybernetic, and organization metaphors that reduce the problem of political legitimacy to sheerly cognitivist sciences. This shift in turn recovers the *embodied rationalities* of everyday living, family survival, health, self-respect, love, and communion. People are aware of the necessary interrelationships among their family, economic, and personal commitments. They judge the benefits of their labors in the productive sector of the body politic in terms of the returns to their familial and personal lives. They are willing to make trade-offs between the demands of family life and the ambitions of their personal and libidinal lives. In short, people have a fairly complex understanding of their corporate lives that is not reducible to the single pattern of utilitarian or decisionistic reasoning that governs calculations in the economic sector.

By differentiating the three levels of the body politic, we further separate ourselves from naturalistic accounts of the problem of political legitimacy by introducing a line of ethical development as the fundamental myth of political life. The three levels of family, economic, and personal life represent a historical-ethical development of anthropomorphosis and also permit us to identify contradictions or constraints and regressions in the body politic. Thus, we can identify alienation as a complex phenomenon that affects not only the productive body but also the bio- and libidinal bodies. Conversely, alienation is not solved merely by satisfying organic needs or by the smooth engineering of productive relations, since these do not meet the demands of the libidinal body. By the same token, we cannot abstract the dreams of libidinal life from our commitments to familial and economic life. A critical theory of the legitimacy problem in the body politic is a constitutive theory simultaneously of social development and of popular recognition of the places where this development is blocked or deteriorating.

The paradox of modern corporate culture is that it panders to the libidinal body, titillating and ravishing its sensibilities, while at the same time it standardizes and packages libidinal responses to its products. In North America the libidinal body politic is the creature of the corporate culture and its celebration of the young, white, handsome, heterosexual world of health and affluence. In this sense, it reflects an unhealthy distortion of the community's political life and a denial of the community's failure to cope with the poor, the sick, the aged, the ugly, and

81

the black. Everything that fails to conform to the image of sub-urb-inanity has to be segregated and pushed into the ghettos of race, poverty, crime, and insanity. It is therefore natural that political struggles over integration in the affluent-racist context of corporate capitalism take on the imagery of white rape, black power, women's liberation and youth protests. A critical theory of political legitimacy, on the other hand, does not discount the rationality of people's ordinary accounts of their political experience in terms of the vocabularies of family, work, and person. It is for this reason that each of the three levels of the body politic is represented in a characteristic institution—the family, the economy, and the person—which is in turn allocated its proper domain of discourse. Although the various institutional and discourse realms of the body politic are analytically differentiated, they may together be said to constitute an evolutionary process in which the congruency of the three discursive orders maximizes the common welfare. Every society needs to reproduce itself biologically, materially, and spiritually. These needs are articulated at the institutional levels of the family, work, and personality where discourse focuses upon relevant notions of well-being, health, suffering, estrangement, and self-expression.

Here I cannot deal with the variety of social science knowledge and alternative socioeconomic institutions that are generated at these various levels of the body politic (we shall examine the functions of biomedical discourse in this regard in Chapter 5). I would point out, however, that the articulation of the libidinal body generates discourse demands that impinge differently upon the institutions of family and work, and that, to date, the institutionalization of these "revolutionary" demands continues to represent a challenge to all modes of scientistic, social, and political knowledge. But even now we can envisage an extension of Habermas's program for the rational justification of an ideal speech community in terms of the specific discursive pragmatics of the tri-level body politic. For such an extension it would be necessary to generate a typology of knowledge and evaluation claims with regard to the bio-body, the productive body, and the libidinal body at each appropriate institutional level, with further criteria for urgency, democratic force, and the like. The business of politics ought, in some way short of authoritarianism, to foster citizens capable of the good life. Therefore, political legitimacy must be grounded in familied contexts and communities of everyday belief and action that regenerate political education without subordinating people to a political science outside the life of the body politic. As Jean Bethke Elshtain observes:

> To attain and affirm an ideal of family life as the locus of humanization is, contrary to certain unreflective radical orthodoxies, to put pressure upon social structures and arrangements, not to affirm them. For to the extent that the public world, with all its political, economic, bureaucratic force, invades and erodes the private sphere, it, not the private world, should be the target of the social rebel and the feminist critic. To promote a politics of displacement that further erodes the terms of the private sphere and all that stands between us and a course of power or market-ridden definition of all of life, is to repress discourse on public, political issues even as one simultaneously takes the symptoms of its destructive effects as "good news" that radical change is just around the corner.[15]

To start on a positive program, let us insist upon anthropomorphism and familism as the root values of political discourse seeking to correct the twin excesses of neo-individualism and statism. To supply meaning and value to the identities, decisions, and interpretations generated in the social system as a quasi-natural environment of public life, the following propositions may be asserted in defense of a familied politics:

(1) Human beings become human in families;
(2) The human family is the foundation of all civil and political life;
(3) The human family is the first cradle of intelligence, common sense, love, and justice;
(4) Political familism does not invite retribalism; rather, it repoliticizes the split between our public and private lives;

83

(5) Maternalism and feminism are properly defenses of the family against the state;

(6) Each family owes to every other human family the right to posterity;

(7) Every family is a witness to the integrity or holiness of the human family.

As Elshtain insists, it can never be too late to rebuild the human family in the interest of fortifying our public life. Indeed, every premature pronouncement of the family's end can only strengthen the state at the expense of those very individuals who place their hope in the socioeconomic processes that lead to defamilization.[16] We have been caught up in a curious mixture of commercialism and welfarism that has sold us the ideal of nuclear family, in a form suburbanized and standardized to the point of inanity. It is this family haven which has collapsed, thrown itself into the arms of the law, psychoanalysis, and medicine. It has nonetheless been used as a model for working-class and marginalized families, though their ways of holding together and coming apart are different. In short, we cannot overlook that the family has been stripped of many of its social functions and reduced to a phase in the lives of individuals whose primary goals are found in school, work, and consumption. Indeed, many of those individuals turned away from the absurd privatization of the family in order to restore intimacy and personality in the political realm, as I noted in my remarks about the body politic during the revolutionary sixties.

The actual history of these developments is largely still to be written.[17] Their future is something to which we must try to contribute. We can do so only by first grasping the central problem of the family's place in the body politic. *We are experiencing a massive shift in our conception of where and how people are to be produced.* A few decades ago such a statement would have raised the horrible vision of an animal farm, a state-medical hatchery in which familied life was a lost memory, a dream punishable by the state guardians. Today we cannot imagine the family outside of the therapeutic state.[18] At the same time, our commercial imagination exploits the family as a haven, madhouse, and a gadget station used by loosely connected relatives, as we shall see in the following chapters. Here we must consider further how we understand the institutional context of the processes of defamilization and civic privacy, which undermine the public and critical intelligence of the family as a vital element in any democracy.

Because capitalism desires, in terms of its own technological myth, to replace human beings with machines, it is driven, however faultily, to try to replace familied society and labor with a consumer or service society. The latter is underwritten by its industrial, legal, and medical technology and a variety of neo-individualist ideologies that seek to reshape our notions of men, women, and children, from familied beings into beings whose rights and duties are defined through the therapeutic state. In such a state the political animal is more of an animal than a political creature since the therapeutic state increases civic privacy at the expense of public life. What I have in mind here refers to more than the historical accumulation of goods and services by the household since early capitalism. What is involved is a sociolegal redefinition of the family for the consumption tasks of late capitalism. A major pedagogic and therapeutic switch is involved, in which family attitudes are "engineered" on behalf of the industrial, commercial, and state system of late capitalism. The ordinary family is increasingly subjected to degradation in favor of the family wise in consumption. This involves the degradation of household work, cooking, cleaning, caring in any way that does not bring the family into the orbit of industry, commerce, and professionalism. Simultaneously, the family that is wired into such commercialism and professionalism in the delivery of its functions is elevated. The result, of course, is that the family again splits. *The bourgeois family, whose professional members service themselves in saving the working-class family, becomes the principal circuit of defamilized and feminized discourse upon family health, education, and welfare.* Thus children's health, education and consumer awareness are the discursive channels for the reorientation of the family to the new demands of late capitalism. Bourgeois feminism and the legal, medical, and educational professions, as well as commercial advertising, combine to subordinate the family "patriarch" to his more en-lightened women and children. Stuart Ewen notes:

> In the death of patriarchy, both libertarians and business shared an interest. Yet their interests were at odds with one another. . . . The commodified answers to the questions of "how to live" began to take on a distinctive character. Utilizing the collective image of the family, the ads in their contribution to mass culture did their best to deny that collectively. Each aspect of the family *collective*— the source of decision making, the locus of child rearing, the things which elicited affectionate response—all of these now pointed outward toward the world of commodities for their direc-tion. Corporate America had begun to define itself as *the father of us all*.[19]

It is easy to recall endless advertisements, comic strips, car-toons, kids' movies, and family movies that dramatize the end of the patriarchal family and its surrender to *consumer matriarchy* sponsored by pseudopaternalist corporations. These scenarios have made Hollywood America the symbol of freedom for mil-lions of people whose families, marriages, and communities kept their noses to the grindstone of authority and scarcity.[20] The beseiged family and its wayward antics are the staple of American lawlessness smiled upon by American law, itself so often the clown in the comedy. In reality, the American family is as much exploited in these scenes as are the still grim indus-trial and monotonous suburban settings that furnish their back-ground. The tragicomedy, however, is played out differently in the towns and in the country, in the middle and upper classes and in working-class, immigrant families, resulting in huge problems of public health and morality, of criminality and ig-norance which beset the ideology of individual self-devel-opment. These, however, provide for a double response by the therapeutic state, at once reinforcing neo-individualism while simultaneously professionalizing and bureaucratizing the soci-olegal practices that correct for its failures.[21] Again, in this the various discourses of scientism, individualism, defamilism, and feminism are subtly interwoven.

As I see it, the shift from early to late capitalism has involved a double strategy of sociolegal redefinition of familism and feminism, leading to the emergence of a new biopolitical economy suited to the needs of liberal welfare-state capitalism. This shift may be roughly summarized in terms of the following stages:

(1) *Pre-industrial family economy*: farm and handicraft work employing the whole family.

(2) *Early capitalism*
    (a) the family is moved into the factory;
    (b) the family is legislated out of the factory; and
    in the bourgeois family
    (c) women are feminized; and
    (d) their children are moralized, while in the working class
    (e) women are feminized but work; and
    (f) their children are moralized, receive some schooling, and soon work.

(3) *Late Capitalism*
    (a) the factory is moved into the family, i.e. consumption provides the reasons for work;
    (b) consumption is feminized and infantilized;
    (c) women's bodies are feminized for work and consumption;
    (d) in both the bourgeois family and the working-class family, the legal and medical sciences are the common source of defamilism and feminism; and
    (e) the welfare state legislates transfer payments to augment the working-class family wage into a social wage; while
    (f) the social sciences provide a legal, administrative, and therapeutic culture in which the twin discourses of defamilism and feminism are floated for all classes.

Despite the Marxist and feminist critique of the family as a reproductive committee of the bourgeoisie and the state, there

87

still remains the analytic task of seeing how divergent discursive strategies developed around the family as a bulwark against the state and simultaneously as the factor that limits criticism and revolt directed against the social order. In other words, the liberal bourgeois conception of state and economic relations meant that the bourgeoisie had to find a solution to the problem of pauperism without generating socialism even though granting rights to work, education, and welfare. Simultaneously, the bourgeoisie had to find a new basis for social commitment on the part of the masses while excluding them from political participation. As Jacques Donzelot shows, two strategies of control came to be preferred: (a) philanthropy and (b) medicine-hygiene. The two strategies were designed to transform the family into a buffer against pauperism on the one hand, by shoring up the practice of family savings and family assistance, and against irresponsible patriarchy on the other, by defending standards of health and morality due to children. Thus from both sides the family became the focus of philanthropic and therapeutic strategies designed to raise its reproductive potential with respect to the economy and the social order without absolute state interference. By the same token, the family was saved by having its autonomy reduced vis-à-vis the therapeutic state, which served the liberal bourgeois concept of society without socialism. It is no accident, then, that in certain respects the laws on divorce go hand in hand with state laws that undermine patriarchal and familial authority over children: the liberalization of the marriage contract is a trade-off for the state's becoming the parent of last resort. Jacques Donzelot writes:

> the modern family is not so much an institution as a *mechanism*. It is through the disparity of the familial configurations (the working class and bourgeois bipolarity), the variances between individual interests and the family interest, that this mechanism operates. Its strength lies in a social *architectonics* whose characteristic feature is always to couple an exterior intervention with conflicts or differences of potential within the family: the protection of poor children which allowed for the destruction of the family as an island of resistance; the privileged alliance of the doctor and the educator

with the wife for developing procedures of savings, educational promotion and so on. The procedures of social control depend much more on the complexity of intrafamilial relationships than on its complexes, more on its craving for betterment than on the defense of its acquisitions (private property, judicial rigidity). A wonderful mechanism, since it enables the social body to deal with marginality through a near-total dispossession of private rights, and to encourage positive integration, the renunciation of the question of political right through the private pursuit of well-being.[22]

We have always to remember that the tendencies I am describing are never in practice wholly congruent with one another. Thus it is possible to see much family law as having delivered married women from the authority of their husbands, restoring child custody to them and releasing them from sexual monogamy.[23] These changes have considerably altered the intrafamilial status of wives. But since, while the state holds out on day care services, women continue to be weak wage earners, women's rights in family law terms do not match the structural realities of the working women's economy. It is therefore a difficult matter to decide upon the extent to which the state oppresses women rather than men. Indeed, the question has no general answer in this form. It can be approached only relative to specific historical stages and policies of capitalism and the liberal state. The ideological function of welfare, social work, and social policy as state apparatuses has been noted by Elizabeth Wilson. The existence of this function, however, does not imply conspiracy on the part of the state or of the bourgeoisie, as I see it. Capitalist society consists of competing and incongruent interests whose group and class affiliations are modified by the ideology of the public good. The position of women, children, and the nuclear family varies with respect to these conflicting claims. According to Wilson, "social policy is simply one aspect of the capitalist state, an acceptable face of capitalism, and social welfare policies amount to no less than the *State organization of domestic life*. Women encounter state repression within the very bosom of the family. This may seem paradoxical when the ideology of individualism and private property that has grown with capitalism has stressed the sanctity of family privacy. But in many ways the Welfare State, like the position of women, is full of paradox and contradiction."[24] Thus the welfare state makes a great effort through social work and psychiatric practice to keep child care in the home, whereas it is determined to move such health services as pre- and postnatal care, birthing, birth control, and abortion, along with old age and death, out of the home. Ultimately, however, the tendency of the therapeutic state is to increase its power over the body politic, as we shall see in the last two chapters.

CHAPTER FOUR

CONSUMER BODIES

IN THIS chapter I want to return to the most familiar image of the body, the body that has *needs*. Between birth and death, we do many things simply to maintain the body as the instrument of much else we seek. For the moment neglecting those intrauterine needs that are present even from the time of conception and leaving aside those that are present even in the process of dying, we can think of life in between these points as the ceaseless pursuit of satisfactions pressed upon us by our bodily condition. We need food, drink, clean air, rest, shelter, clothing, a certain standard of public health and safety; and we need these things both to sustain life and to reproduce it in a reasonably healthy population whose offspring will have a fair chance of survival.

Bodily needs might then be considered *basic* needs—their satisfaction constituting the simple but sound pleasures of living that Plato described for the "first city":

> Let us begin, then, with a picture of our citizens' manner of life, with the provisions we have made for them. They will be producing corn and wine, and making clothes and shoes. When they have built their houses, they will mostly work without their coats or shoes in the summer, and in winter be well shoed and clothed.

For their food, they will prepare flour and barley-meal for knead-ing and baking, and set out a grand spread of loaves and cakes on rushes or fresh leaves. Then they will lie on beds of myrtle-boughs and byrony and make merry with their children, drinking their wine after the feast with garlands on their heads and singing the praises of the gods. So they will live pleasantly together; and a prudent fear of poverty or war will keep them from begetting chil-dren beyond their means.[1]

Ours, however, is an ambivalent legacy. If, in accordance with the Christian tradition, we were to imagine a society ruled by the body, then it too might have looked like the Garden of Eden. But, as we know, the bodies we have are a fallen version of those that Adam and Eve once enjoyed. Having succumbed to Eve's curiosity, our bodies now suffer a life of hard labor, ending in death:

To the woman he said,
   "I will greatly multiply your pain in childbearing;
   in pain you shall bring forth children,
   yet your desire shall be for your husband,
   And he shall rule over you."
and to Adam he said,
   "Because you have listened to the voice of your wife,
   and have eaten of the tree
   of which I commanded you, 'You shall not eat of it',
   cursed is the ground because of you: in toil you shall eat of it
   all the days of your life;
   thorns and thistles it shall bring forth to you;
   and you shall eat the plants of the field.
   In the sweat of your face you shall eat bread
   till you return to the ground, for out of it you were taken;
   you are dust, and to dust you shall return."
                    [Gen. 3:16–19]

We are chained, then, to the alternating pleasures and pains of the body's satisfaction. Now it is clear that in terms of that other biblical injunction, that man should be lord of the earth, we have created a great civilization within which the necessities of life and the conditions of labor and consumption have been refined almost beyond imagination. Intellectual, artistic, scientific, culinary, medical, legal, political, and even military culture expands beyond any level that can be contained by the simple standard of bodily need. Indeed, the proliferation of civilizational or cultural needs has been so overwhelming that it has always provoked religious, moral, and social thinkers to try to find a base line between natural or primary needs and secondary, or excessive and *unnatural* needs. Such efforts to discriminate between primary and secondary needs have been motivated by the problem of good and evil, by the problem of poverty in the midst of plenty, and by a nostalgia for modes of living that seem less egoistic, less competitive and inauthentic than life in societies ruled by the constant drive to accumulate wealth, power, and privilege.

Turning the pages of any modern magazine is enough to cause us to discover that we are still consumed with the problem of *authentic* human needs but quite unable to erase the line between lives that celebrate unlimited affluence and a world of misery where millions still lack rudimentary food and shelter. In either case, the body is the icon of abundance and misery, of dieting and starvation, of sexuality and mutilation. This paradox has provoked a number of attempts to discover a fundamental economic anthropology. In particular, it requires us to rethink the relation between material and symbolic culture already considered in Chapter 2, and I propose now to develop some recent arguments in this direction, while preserving my chosen focus upon the political economy of the body.

The dilemma from which we start is the nature of our own economy. In offering to meet our every need, it seems less to serve us than to enslave us. As John Kenneth Galbraith observes, it is as though our economy were ruled by an evil genius:

Were it so that a man on arising each morning was assailed by demons which instilled in him a passion sometimes for silk shirts, sometimes for kitchenware, sometimes for chamber pots, some-

93

times for orange squash, there would be every reason to applaud the effort to find the goods, however odd, that quenched this flame. But should it be that his passion was the result of his first having cultivated the demons, and should it also be that his effort to allay it stirred the demons to even greater and greater effort, there would be question as to how rational was his solution. Unless restrained by conventional attitudes, he might wonder if the solution lay with more goods or fewer demons.

So it is that if production creates the wants it seeks to satisfy, or if the wants emerge *pari passu* with the production, then the urgency of the wants can no longer be used to defend the urgency of the production. Production only fills a void that it has itself created.[2]

To the ancients, the modern experience would have been no surprise. Indeed, Galbraith's imagery of the demonic forces of unleashed consumption captures the idiocy of any society engaged in the pursuit of order based upon passion. In Plato's *Republic*, for example, it is this tendency that is subdued by making the passions subject to a hierarchy of moral and intellectual pursuits whose fixed relative place guarantees the healthy order of society. In such a system, it would be monstrous to think of the passions, or of the merchant and laboring elements, ruling those who think and defend the social order. Even on the eve of modern society, it appeared convincing to Hobbes that the passion for power could be brought to order only in an authoritarian state that canceled man's pride and fear.[3] In contrast, the remarkable assertion is made in Adam Smith's *Wealth of Nations* that if men would only restrict themselves to trading in their *private passions*, there would result a *public order* more secure than anything church or state could guarantee. Moreover, it was held that church and state would reveal a higher morality by leaving the market free, for if ever morality were to prevail over vice, the economy would collapse and church and state with it. In the words of Mandeville:

For the main design of the Fable, (as it is breefly explain'd in the Moral) is to shew the Impossibility of enjoying all the most elegant

94

Comforts of Life that are to be met with in an industrious, wealthy and powerful Nation, and at the same time be bless'd with all the Virtue and Innocence that can be wish'd for in a Golden Age; from thence to expose the Unreasonableness and Folly of those, that desirous of being an opulent and flourishing People, and wonderfully greedy after all the Benefits they can receive as such, are yet always murmuring at and exclaiming against those Vices and Inconveniencies, that from the beginning of the World to this present Day, have been inseparable from all Kingdoms and States that ever were fam'd for Strength, Riches and Politeness at the same time.[4]

To those of us still puzzled by the variety of good and evil and the inextricable mixture of sense and nonsense in our lives, Mandeville remains a consolation. Yet the fact is that it is precisely in those societies where the economy is highly autonomous that the crown is still disputed between consumption and production. Critics like Galbraith believe that consumption can be made more rational only if we devise rational agenda for production since, despite the theorists of consumer sovereignty and with just a little attention to advertising, it is obvious that consumer needs are generated in the productive sector rather than in the consumer's body, however his or her demons may push. But this dependence effect as such is not responsible for the irrationality of consumer behavior. For, as we shall see, economic anthropology reveals that in every society wants are largely cultural acquisitions. In the case of our own society, therefore, we cannot understand the arrangement of the economic agenda in favor of private consumption over public consumption (except where the latter, for this very reason, is stigmatized as poor relief or welfare benefits even when declared a citizen's right) unless we adopt a *semiological* approach to commodity functions. To repeat an earlier shibboleth, we must try to see what it is that *commodities are good for thinking* as well as what it is they are good for consuming. But taking that latter route gets us into all the difficulties of trying to think apart necessary and unnecessary goods despite the fact that each is in someone's interest to produce and consume. We find ourselves

95

looking for religious, moral, and historical benchmarks that might point to the primacy of necessary and natural consumption as the guide to an economy that would remain subordinate to the overall social order.

In *The Theory of the Leisure Class*, Veblen argued that what confers upon the pursuit of wealth its insatiable nature is not its function of satisfying natural needs so much as its accommodation to the pursuit of an insatiable need for *social prestige*.[5] Social man does not live by bread alone. Socialists have nevertheless managed to read Veblen's message as though it restricted conspicuous consumption to bourgeois man. They have imagined that in so-called primitive societies and in future communist societies the prestige economy would be absent. The other side of the same coin is that capitalists are not free to universalize "status seeking" because we find it functioning in potlatch societies on the Pacific Northwest coast of Canada,[6] in the United States, and even in the Soviet Union. Rather, what the anthropological evidence seems to reveal is that preindustrial societies distinguish between goods and regulate exchanges in a two-tier system: (i) the *subsistence* economy, and (ii) the *prestige* or ceremonial economy. Even among the famous Kwakiutl, subsistence goods played no part in the prestige economy, which was restricted to the accumulation of blankets and large pieces of engraved copper. Where there was an exchange between the two systems it was regulated, as Mary Douglas shows, so that people did not amass subsistence goods at the expense of their neighbors.[7] In fact, it is possible to argue that the prestige economy had, through feasts, a redistributive function, correcting imbalances in the subsistence economy.

In our own economy, we seem unable to distinguish between subsistence and prestige economics.[8] Although we speak of guaranteed minimum-wage levels, the goods upon which this money is spent are not kept separate from the prestige economy, which redefines simple use-values in invidious terms of prestige consumption, style, and class position. So-called transfer payments and most public-sector goods like health and education facilities are regarded as adjustments to their counterparts in the private sector. Consider the trouble we experienced until very recently in redesigning the automobile. If the automobile were merely a means of transportation, the task of recreating smaller, more fuel-efficient cars—not to mention shifting the transportation of people to buses and trains—would be simple. But the automobile is a symbolic good. It is the vehicle not only of bodies but of bodies who value the ideas of privacy and freedom. The automobile is therefore as much a vehicle of individual ideology as of anything else it might carry. To accommodate this automotive ideology, we have subordinated vast amounts of space to roadways and parking areas; we have suburbanized our cities and turned country villages into shopping centers; and we have vastly altered the quality of everyday life with noise, pollution, and loss of life and limb in favor of a machine that promises us youth, beauty, and sexual and social mobility. As a *symbolic vehicle*, therefore, the automobile circulates between the economy of use (transportation) and the economy of prestige (power, energy, style). As such, it is perfectly geared to express the cultural value we place upon technology, private property, individual mobility, sexual rivalry, and social competition. Despite its claims, it is not only the Volvo that is the thinking man's car. In our society all cars are good to think as well as drive. Henri Lefebvre notes: "The car is a status symbol, it stands for comfort, power, authority and speed, *it is consumed as a sign* in addition to its practical use, its various significances involving, intensifying and neutralizing each other as it stands for consumption and consumer symbols, symbolizes happiness and procures happiness by symbols."[9]

We began by trying on the notion that the meeting of simple subsistence needs might give primacy to consumption and thereby make production to meet those needs rational or reasonable. But we have found that as social bodies we are committed to much more than our own biological and material reproduction. As communicative bodies we are involved in the consumption and (re)production of the culture and society we inhabit. We cannot, therefore, treat the economy as a production process set in motion by consumption and determined

97

solely by its material logic. We have to learn to rethink the language of consumption and production in terms of discourse patterns not governed by any simple utilitarian logic. Above all, we have to learn to set aside the logocentric notion of the sovereign consumer assembling utilities according to his/her own rational schedules of need. This is precisely how the *ideological* conception of consumption functions as a myth of bourgeois thought which fetishizes objects no less than its primitive cousins. We cannot say what an American car is without knowing what it is that American society thinks and does with cars. People other than Americans also have their mythologies of the automobile. Consider, for example, Roland Barthes's comment on the Citroën D.S. 19 (there is a play on words involved; D.S. as pronounced in French sounds the same as *déesse*, which means goddess):

> It is obvious that the new Citroën has fallen from the sky inasmuch as it appears at first sight as a superlative *object*. We must not forget that an object is the best messenger of a world above nature: one can easily see in an object at once a perfection and an absence of origin, a closure and a brilliance, a transformation of life onto matter (matter is much more magical than life), and in a word a *silence* which belongs to the realm of fairy tales. The D.S.— the 'Goddess'—has all the features (or at least the public is unanimous in attributing them to it at first sight) of one of those objects from another universe which have supplied fuel for the neomania of the eighteenth century and that of our own science-fiction: the *Déesse* is *first and foremost* a new *Nautilus*.[10]

As an object, therefore, the automobile functions as a token in a larger discourse. The same is true of needs. We cannot restrict needs to the biobody. Indeed, as we shall see, even bioneeds are symbolically mediated to function in the larger discourse of the medicalized society and its therapeutic ideology. Incidentally, I am not recommending the study of "distorting" sociopsychological and sociosomatic effects upon otherwise rational economic behavior. Rather I am proposing to rethink the categories of consumption, production, and distribution in terms of the semiotics or *rhetoric of commodities* as discourse types signifying a variety of social domains ranging from subsistence to fantasy. Jean Baudrillard has dealt with the same issue:

> The logic of exchange is therefore primordial. In some ways, the individual is nothing (any more than the object we were talking about at first), and a given language (of words, women, or commodities) is what exists first, as a social form in respect of which there are no individuals since it is a structure of exchange. This structure arises from a logic of differentiation working simultaneously on two levels:
> 1. It differentiates the human elements of exchange into pairs that are not individuated but distinct and tied by the rule of exchange.
> 2. It differentiates the material elements of exchange into distinct, therefore meaningful, elements.
>
> The same is true of communication in language. It is also true of goods and products. Consumption is exchange. It is here that we need to introduce a complete revolution in the analysis of consumption. *No language exists because of an individual need to speak* (which would pose the doubly insolvable problem of grounding this need in the individual, and then of articulating it in a possible system of exchange). Language exists, first of all—not as an absolute, autonomous *system* but as a structure of exchange contemporaneous with meaning itself and within which the individual articulates what he wants to say. In the same fashion, "consumption" does not exist because of an objective need to consume, or some final intention in the subject vis-à-vis the object. Through a system of exchange there develops the social production of differentiated materials and of a code of meanings and established values. The functionality of goods and individual needs supervenes, adjusting itself to, rationalizing, and repressing these fundmental structural mechanisms.[11]

Let us glance at Plato's *Republic* once again. In the construction of his perfect state, Plato distinguishes between a first and a second city. He begins by imagining a first city, in which people eat and drink simply and do little more than is required to sustain and reproduce their families. For some reason this situation is unstable, and the people begin to expand their wants. In the second city there is no simple way of relating decisions to the features of the natural setting. Desires are complex, commodities abound, and good and evil cease to be distinguishable without the specific work of philosophy and politics, which henceforth must rule the body and subjugate the economy that characterizes the modern world. Yet the economy remains a very moral order. It claims to be in the service of worldwide human need, and it is the setting for displays of creativity, intelligence, and foresight that it in turn rewards as evidence of its own good auspices. The modern economy makes a powerful claim to be the sole source of the good life and the principal training ground of the moral qualities required for its successful production, if not consumption. Looked at in this way, the stratification system, so far from being an evil, acts as a moral screen, a device for representing the stages in the good life rather than any obstacle to its pursuit.

Marx argued that all production is social.[12] I want to include in the notion of production not just the expenditure of physical labor but also the employment of every technique of the body in a unified field of production and consumption. By this I mean that we must regard the *productive body* as an extension of the economy and not simply as a factor of production like labor. Like its labor power, the fetishizations of the productive body exist only in a market economy capable of reifying its stress, relaxation, health, illness, beauty, spontaneity, and sexuality. The reification of the body into productive sectors concerned with its own production and consumption integrates and redistributes the body throughout the social division of labor. Thus the productive body is not a factor of production in the way that Marx thought of land, labor, and capital. The productive body is integrated into the division of labor both internally—for example, through modern medicine—and externally—for example, through fashion and cosmetics. Thus the productive body is both an extension and an intensification of the space and activity of the modern economy. It is not simply that the economy expropriates the labor of the body, subjecting it to pain in its tasks and to an unsatisfactory standard of living in return for its wages. Consumers can be taught to disvalue their biological bodies entirely, except as those bodies are reappraised in the willing consumption of industrially mediated experience, looks, attitudes, and characters. The modern economy is able to control the socially significant points of entry and exit in the life cycle, prematurely declaring young persons worldly-wise and old persons obsolescent. Every physical, mental, and emotional need of persons will eventually be reified as a chemical agent or professional service. Thus, unless we learn to resist and to refuse, what was once self-knowledge and personal identity will amount to nothing other than the consumerised capacity to refer a residual self to the appropriate externalization of the productive body.

The most massive exploitation of the body occurs whenever the economy teaches us to disvalue it in its natural state and to revalue it only once it has been sold grace, spontaneity, vivaciousness, bounce, confidence, smoothness, and freshness. Here the economy is a principal socializing agency in those techniques of the body that display the cultural values of youth, aggression, mobility, and sociability. By the same token, it is obliged to hide the ordinary condition of men, women, and children. As life becomes more sedentary and less physically demanding (though a certain myth is at work here—notice how many people are tired!), the economy is able to sell physical activity as recreation, fitness, and sport. The vicarious consumption of bodily experiences is a further characteristic of mass society. It extends from sport to the theater, and thereby makes violence and sexuality principal ingredients of these commodities. The more the modern family is geared to consumption, the more it needs to divide into wage earners who separate sexuality and reproduction. Thus the female body must be deromanticized and made solely the instrument of rational, that is, contractual associations. Trusting to the pill, young women's bodies are made mobile for work, high-rise living, and adventure. Physical hazards, ranging from cancer to rape, are all part of this bodily complex that sings its appeal to the young self-possessed women of the cigarette and perfume world, as we shall see in more detail further on.

The modern economy, then, engages us in an enormous expansion of wants and desires while claiming to satisfy these desires in ethical ways.[13] The two sides of this equation are production and consumption. From economics we receive only a general notion of the human labor that goes into work and consumption. We know that much work even today requires bodily labor, physical and nervous pain. We know less about consumption, as is evident from the largely metabolic metaphor we use to describe our relations to commodities, many of which have little to do with eating or drinking and whose use can hardly be understood by means of any such analogy. I believe we need to think of the *work of consumption* in order to begin to understand what is required of us in the collection, display, and disposal of commodities that service the collective representation of a scientific and technical culture. It is essential that the consumer is not born but is produced by *anxiety-inducing* processes that teach him and her to want to want things that service needs which arose in the first place only from commercial invention. Few people have sensibilities more than equal to the capacity of the modern economy to produce discriminations of need in, for example, the consumption of hi-fi equipment. Millions of consumers are conscripted to the labor of learned discontent from their earliest childhood. In North America and Europe it is the practice of the large stores to distribute to private homes great catalogues of desire that far exceed the longings of a Faustian soul. Children apprentice themselves to these manuals at first for Christmas, but later learn that the Christmas spirit should be kept for every shopping day. The child's imagination is both destroyed and re-created by these catalogues. They are, however, essential to the family economy, inasmuch as, for the children, they serve to integrate the parents' labor with the general exchange of commodities their labor presupposes. At the same time, the catalogues keep consumption ahead of production, and so the family is subject to injurious strain among its members and in comparison with other families. As a result, consumers must learn *economic sacrifice*, that is to say, everyone must learn that it is imperative to keep up with the economy's futuristic production of needs and satisfactions by putting aside present needs of the self in favor of the future self or its family. As Richard Sennett and Jonathan Cobb put it: "The result of this, we believe, is that the activities which keep people moving in a class society, which make them seek more money, more possessions, higher-status jobs, do not originate in a materialistic desire, or even sensuous appreciation of things, but out of an attempt to restore a psychological deprivation that class structure has effected in their lives. In other words, *the psychological motivation instilled by a class society is to heal a doubt about the self rather than create more power over things and other persons in the world.*"[14]

Although the economics of consumption is only partially illuminated by the bodily metaphor with which it is glossed—though perhaps the light is equal to that shed on the supply side by the bodily metaphor of production—it is nevertheless worthwhile remarking upon what is lost in ignoring the metaphor's implications. Economists assume, for example, that whereas production is painful or thoughtful, consumption is easy, pleasant, and costless. They can hold this premise only because even when concerned with consumption economists still operate with a disembodied subject, an abstract pain/pleasure calculator whose own operation costs nothing. *There are no perplexed, harassed, tired, disappointed, crazy consumers in economics.* Above all, there are no housewives, husbands, children, old folk, or families for whom consumer sovereignty is an irony, given the way they have to make household decisions in the market and work place. In short, economists have entirely overlooked the work of consumption. The bewildering range of consumer choices, of brands, weights, and ingredients, not to mention the choices in styles, locations, and scenarios of living, relaxing, entertaining, and the like is apt to call for considerable effort from the consumer—so much, in fact, that without the help of servants he or she may be overwhelmed by the burdens of consumption. Hence the further imposition placed upon us by self-service establishments, which exact considerable labor from us.

In the middle class, where consumption is a heavy obligation—and where servants are hardly obtainable—we find an elaborate "role-set" in which the husband/wife team serves as janitor, gardener, cook, chauffeur, host, parent, lover, and friend in a single day. Galbraith is virtually alone among economists in noticing the reality of the household economy and in particular the tasks of women, hitherto ignored by classical economics.[15] Economists presume upon the cryptoservant role of women in the administration of the household consumption process. They may or may not have noticed its celebration in advertising. But in their calculations of GNP, they hide the female production of household goods and services. Galbraith writes:

> In few other matters has the economic system been so successful in establishing values and molding resulting behavior to its needs as in the shaping of womanly attitude and behavior. And . . . the economic importance of the resulting achievement is great. Without women to administer it, the possibility of increasing consumption would be sharply circumscribed. With women assuming the tasks of administration, consumption can be more or less indefinitely increased. In very high income households this administration becomes . . . an onerous task. But even here expansion is still possible; at these levels women tend to be better educated and better administrators. And the greater availability of divorce allows of a measure of trial and error to obtain the best. Thus it is women in their cryptoservant role who make an indefinitely increasing consumption possible. As matters now stand, (and for as long as they so stand), it is their supreme contribution to the modern economy.[16]

Having observed so much, Galbraith nevertheless fails to see that it is one thing to expose the economic ideology of the consumer woman and quite another to treat the modern family as though it were nothing but a consumption factory in which the formerly productive males have lost any need for a consuming female counterpart. Having observed the reduction of the male productive function, Galbraith goes right on to argue for female independence as something that can be acquired only through control over a wage earned in the market place.[17] Surely, the larger economic and political phenomenon is *the consumerization of males and females alike*, with productive economic decisions removed to the higher levels of the economy. This split is not altered by admitting women into either level of the economy, at least for as long as we retain some line between the consumption imperative and earning a wage. Whether or not he sees this problem, Galbraith in effect moves his argument for the emancipation of women to the thesis that as the economy shifts from the secondary to tertiary stages, that is, to the predominance of services over things, the female administration of thing consumption will decline, services being self-consuming and requiring little administration. But since services tend to be either labor-intensive or intellect-intensive, it is difficult to see how they assure emancipation for anyone employed in them.

In my view, it is necessary for women to rethink the administration of consumption from the standpoint of the familied body, that is, from the standpoint of women's bodies and those of their husbands and children. This means that women must also rethink the embodied relations between the economy, the state, law, and medicine, as I have tried to show in the previous chapter. Because such a task is so tremendous, women will be led away from it to the extent that they subscribe to the belief that freedom, rationality, and independence may be achieved merely by going to work. Workers do not typically find these effects in their lives solely from going to work. Moreover, they are generally driven to buying back hastily the time they have lost at work in the form of those instant ingredients of clever products which they must afford to compensate themselves for working. These connections are difficult to understand. Their analysis is only clouded by attributing their structural nature to the willfulness of men considered as the natural enemies of women. As embodied beings, none of us can be indifferent to the social fates of men and women alike, and each of us must share what we can understand about the political economy that shapes our lives.

There is a good deal of evidence to show the increasing bodily and emotional stress that the working woman ("girl") encounters in the wonderful world of work. Of course, there is a solicitous drug industry ready to offer women relief from "their" troubles, and we can expect political pressure upon the therapeutic state to offer women more "welfare," and more "social security." Meantime, women, despite a general decline in the habit of smoking, seem more resistant than men to health warnings on this subject. This is, I think, evidence of the social contradictions in their lives, which find expression in the pleasure, more risky than risqué, of smoking as a compensation for the mixed joys of working in other industries. It may therefore be useful to analyze how we experience the productive body in the everyday economy by examining the text of a fairly well known series of cigarette advertisements (Winston's "I smoke for only one reason"). Such advertisements generally focus upon the body of a young woman or a young man, and sometimes upon an androgynous image. The message is that sex is competitive and competition is sexual. Hence the Winston text conveys the notion that a person can be on top of the commodity world ("I don't smoke a brand to be like everybody else") and that his or her body is the means to such success. The body is at once a resource and the sanction for socioeconomic success. The sanction of success is revealed in the body's beauty and confidence. The woman pictured—let us call her "Jane"—is beautiful, her hair is well groomed, her clothes are just right, her jewelry and accessories are in perfect taste. The success that comes from smoking the right cigarette shows through in yet other goods of Jane's body—its beauty, its stylishness, its knowingness. Jane knows what she wants: "I smoke for only one reason." The text appeals to the new political culture where women know what they want and get it. Having only one reason in this life would indeed constitute a really masterly consumer achievement. Every day and all day each of us experiences a continuous environmental solicitation as to what to do with his or her life. It is fantastic: Jane might have spent today in Florida, or in Spain or Portugal. She could have stayed in the best hotels thanks to a credit card, or have bought a car, or have eaten anywhere she fancies. The economy of desire is endlessly sending us in search of this or that. Thus the person who wants only one thing and is prepared to stand by it in the commodity world is a master, a consumer sovereign.

The text continues: "I don't smoke a brand to be like everybody else." But, of course, the industrial world is possible only on the basis of a mass society. Mass production creates loyalties to brands which are our compromise between personality and anonymity. You and I all wear some variant of roughly the same clothing. We are able to make only minimal variations in our dress in order to call it our own. So here is Jane—a woman quite unlike anyone else. If that were truly the cigarette's appeal, then Winstons would cost ten dollars or more a pack. But they have to be smoked by enough people to be bought inexpensively and, at the same time, those who buy them have to think that they are exclusive. Thus we might include in surplus value the fantasy we supply to give the commodity its life, in addition to the labor spent on its production and consumption. Surplus value is increasingly the fantasy work that we contribute on behalf of the system to make the system appear to be at the service of individuals: "I smoke because I enjoy it." With so much of the advertisement claiming that the smoker is a confident and successful person, it is possible then to claim that the enjoyment of cigarettes is more like self-controlled behavior than a mere whim. "Super King's extra length gives me an extra smooth taste that's real. Real taste—and real pleasure—are what smoking's all about, Winston is for real." There follows an inserted text that says, "Warning: The Surgeon General has determined that cigarette smoking is dangerous to your health." This text reminds us of the biological body, but makes its worries our business whereas its desires are being exploited by big business. The text warns us that smoking as a biochemical process is injurious. It drowns this message, however, reducing it to an afterthought that is outweighed by the offer of self-assurance in an unsure world—all purchased as simply as buying a packet of cigarettes promising reality, enjoyment, style, and distinction. The advertisement invites us to risk our biological life on behalf of our social life. Thus Jane's self-assurance also services a rebellious conformity.

The advertisement I have analyzed wishes to portray self-certainty as the best of living, for which the productive body is the supreme resource. If we look at the picture, we might be tempted to say that Jane is smoking only for relaxation. There are no factories in the background, no husband, and no children. So Jane is absolutely herself; she is young and she is beautiful. She is fabulously available. She is free. She might be married, she might not. Jane is a goddess. Yet everything about her, by making use of her beauty and her youth, puts her to work. Though her carefree setting makes Jane seem to be absolutely free, in fact she is carefully dressed up. One must recall all the work that goes into her hair to get it to look as it does in the advertisement. Nobody has hair like that. It is the product of a huge chemical industry selling hair work to millions of women who hope to look as though they haven't done any work at all, to look as free as the air. Jane is engaged in a similar conspiracy. In working on behalf of these industries, so far from being free, she is as busy and in as much trouble as she could be in that nice picture.

The same is true of Jane's equally well-known counterpart, Marlborough Man. The lone cowboy is wedded to nothing but the brand of cigarettes he smokes. Despite his apparent freedom, Marlborough Man's insides wear a deeper mark (as the Surgeon General warns) than do any of the steers we imagine him roping in. Thus the wild west and the smoke-stack American are blended on behalf of the tobacco industry's survival, whatever its cost to us.

My analysis of the advertisement also enables us to see that commodities are not just what they seem to be—they represent *commitments* to the institutions of society in which we are daily members and to which we are committed almost from the moment we rise from our beds to start eating on their behalf, seeing, feeling, and moving around, in settings, fabrics, colors that celebrate our modern, clean, and convenient world. Thus the modern home is increasingly disembodied, as it were, and thereby decathected. As more machines are installed, a woman's world becomes a matter of pressing buttons so that it is less likely her children will love the embodied routines of family life. Living spaces are opened up in a modern home, and the settings in which we live are minor modifications of a general setting one could find at the Home Exhibition. Thus the most intimate places of our living are presented as anyone's place. Anybody is a potential buyer of our home. As an extension of this publicity, the body and its most self-involving conducts are required to be as visible as possible, as all our bathroom, bedroom, and toiletry commercials witness. In this way, we see how it is that the body is a resource for the commercial aesthetics of a democratic society, one of the most extraordinary sights of which is sweating men and women, bending and bowing to the ideal figure that will forever elude them.

Of course we do not literally consume automobiles, television sets, furniture, houses, clothing, cosmetics, and entertainment. Does this mean, then, that they do not involve our bodies? Rather, we must ask, how do they involve our bodies? We need to clothe, house, and transport our bodies, just as we need to feed them. But there are now very particular relationships between these necessities. Thus, as urban centers lie at greater distances from the centers of food production, food is increasingly processed and packaged for its life in transport and supermarkets. This secondary necessity involves the use of chemical ingredients in food which may reduce its nutritional value, and even make it harmful. To eat such food might now be considered *work*, risking an industrial injury such as cancer on behalf of the urban/industrial complex. Along the same lines, consider white middle-class reproductive behavior. The event of birth is embedded in the overall contractual rationality of our society, whose instrumentality, in this case, is the chemical agency of the pill. In the condom/pill culture, we have two technical instruments that make it possible to consider the acts of entry and lovemaking rational, inasmuch as lovemaking may be combined with a decision to have or not to have children. Thus, in the modern world we are able to make the womb and the vagina places of *contractual order*. We can in fact construe our bodies, particularly the womb, in terms of political tactics, so that women may claim to have a right to their own bodies, and thereby absolute rights over the fetus, as is claimed by proabortionists. By the same token, however, the therapeutic state may legislate embryo rights and uterine standards. Sexuality and reproduction can now be separated or combined, like all other elements of role-specific conduct, according to rational decision. Thus a seemingly natural bodily function is involved in at least three systems of power, which claim to make the event of reproduction an orderly affair. It is necessary to allow for claims of religious institutions that have long had a say-so about reproduction, and for the views of a scientific culture, inasmuch as its contraceptive techniques service self-determination, and for political institutions, inasmuch as we are now attracted by sexual equality and its implications for other social institutions.

It may also be argued, however, that the so-called sexual revolution is actually a phenomenon of even deeper levels of *bodily alienation*, inasmuch as it makes work out of sex, produces new levels of anxiety over orgasmic quotas and insatiability, or else, like the coffee break, becomes part of the hurried relaxation of ever busier people. In short, the so-called sexual revolution in its commodity forms may be only part of the increasing *stress culture* of Western industrial society. In fact, there is already evidence that as women emancipate themselves, which broadly means assuming the stresses of the work world males have allegedly made for themselves, their smoking, drinking, and self-tranquilizing behavior also increase, as does their criminality.

All these phenomena require us to engage in some basic thinking about the fundamental bond between people and society, if we are not simply to argue ideologically or on the basis of bits and pieces of social science information whose limits are unknown to us. We need to rethink our basic conceptions of society, persons, family, and political institutions, and in doing so to learn that the social sciences are in themselves highly questionable sources of information, values, and social policy. In this connection, there is much discussion regarding the relation between biology and sociology.[18] The arguments can be quite heated. Some scientists find the powers of the human organism to be largely contained in its biogram. They consider that social institutions can do very little to change—and perhaps can also damage—the genetic codes that are the basis for human behavior. Thus, *biosociologists*, as we might call them, look upon the cultural variety in human behavior as a relatively unimportant modification of biological factors which they consider to constitute the proper study of man. Sociologists and anthropologists are not at all happy with the biosociologists. They consider biosociology a serious threat to the patient efforts of social scientists to locate the forces that limit human intelligence, freedom, creativity, and well-being in powerful but modifiable social institutions. They mistrust the arguments of the biosociologists, seeing in them an effort once again to naturalize human inequalities, whether of intelligence, gender, or race. We may nonetheless still speak of most social scientists as *sociobiologists*. That is to say, they would not deny certain limiting and enabling capacities of the human organism. But they consider these effects to be so largely integrated with psychosocial culture as to deserve only residual consideration in determining the strategy of the social sciences.

It may seem surprising to find scientists at each other's throats, although the history of science ought to dispel the image of serene objectivity it generally tries to convey to the public lest its authority be diminished. The fact is that it is very difficult to establish norms of human conduct even at the level of anatomy and physiology, let alone for intelligence, emotions, eating, dress, child care, sexuality—which all involve behavior subject to rich cultural, literary, artistic, and religious definition. Today there are even arguments to the effect that much of human biology, for example, gender and sexual behavior, is subject to purely political definition. In fact, it is argued that any theoretical or methodological approach to human behavior that ignores the political definition of the settings and comportment required of us is part of the repression that the social sciences ought to be fighting. From this point of view the infighting between different sociological approaches is regarded as a criminal waste of time.

Thus, Juliet Mitchell has argued more cautiously that we need to distinguish a number of factors at work in the history of women's inferior social position, rather than contend simply that their biological status diminishes their value at work while increasing it in reproductive relations. In order to provide a stage-specific historical analysis of the structure of exploitative relations ruling women, she proposed (in the mid-1960s) to speak of four structures determining women's social value: (1) production; (2) reproduction; (3) sex; and (4) the socialization of children. Women's emancipation cannot be treated as a sort of idealization of socialist freedom. It requires specific legislation in the field of equal work conditions and remuneration, contraceptive practices, the mutuality of sexual experience, and new agencies for child socialization:

> In practical terms this means a coherent system of demands. The four elements of women's condition cannot merely be considered each in isolation; they form a structure of specific inter-relations. The contemporary bourgeois family can be seen as a triptych of sexual, reproductive, and socializatory functions (the women's world) embraced by production (the men's world)—precisely a structure which in the final instance is determined by the economy. The exclusion of women from production—social human activity—and their confinement to a monolithic condensation of functions in a unity—the family—which is precisely unified in the *natural* part of each function, is the root cause of the contemporary *social* definition of women as *natural* beings. Hence the main thrust of any emancipation movement must still concentrate on the economic element—the entry of women fully into public industry.[19]

It should be possible now, in view of my earlier arguments, to understand how Juliet Mitchell was able to combine the social definition of the *natural* qualities of women with an analysis of the *economic interests* in such a definition. It is, however, difficult to evaluate much of the contemporary sexual and economic emancipation of women. In the first place, there are the troubles of token reform. Then, it must be recognized that the women's liberation movement is largely a middle-class, urban, and industrial phenomenon, in which the first-generation beneficiaries are necessarily a small number of already relatively privileged women. At the same time, recognition must be given to the women's movement for challenging gender and sexual stereotypes, and generally for awakening society to the loss of human potential resulting from undervaluing its females. Leaders of the women's movement, however, ought to avoid specious conspiratorial arguments about male supremacy in the economy and polity. Clearly, for most of human history, and still in large areas of the world, most men and their families with them have been and are brutally exploited by a system that has little to do with genital differences but much to do with differences in accumulated wealth and influence. Whatever the difficulties, it now seems certain that the social status of women will continue to be an issue in modern society and that we can expect continuing reforms along several lines—reforms whose achievement would be difficult to imagine without the struggle in which women are presently engaged, in pursuit of something like the following basic civil rights for all women:

(1) the right to equal educational opportunity
(2) the right to equal employment opportunity
(3) the right to sexual equality
(4) the right to control conception
(5) the right to bodily integrity in the widest sense to cover rape, pornography, abuse, and medical exploitation.

Gaining such rights involves considerable changes in familial and male-female relations, as well as changes in schools, in the churches, and in all places of employment. Like any process of social change, moving in these new directions is likely to take more time than is allowed for in their rhetorical proclamation. Tradition, ethnicity, social class—these alone are powerfully resistant forces in human behavior. In turn, we cannot entirely overlook the psychobiological factors in human and familial relations. A number of important issues facing the women's movement have been raised by Alice Rossi, a sociologist who is far from unsympathetic to the general problem: (1) To what extent will the majority of women, who have not experienced consciousness-raising, use such facilities as abortion centers, child care centers and communal housing? (2) To what extent can the issue of homosexual solidarity be identified with the issue of heterosexual mutuality in the general population? (3) Are there not in fact neurohormonal differences between males and females that provide underlying dispositions toward respectively more competitive and more nurturant behavior? (4) In promoting the clitoral orgasm over the vaginal orgasm, are not feminists insisting upon a separation that is false to the integration of sexuality, reproduction, and lactation?[20]

Women certainly have much to fight for. It is a pity, therefore, how often feminists speak of women in traditional societies as submissive, repeating a prejudice of sociology when in fact modern society possesses equally potent techniques for gaining the submission of women. For example, many traditional women will only smile at the modern discovery of the merits of breast feeding and natural childbirth. As Rossi's own remarks make clear, the nursing and medical professions, which require a passive body as the docile object of their practice, are the greatest of forces working for the submission of women. Moreover, it is important to recall that even in modern society there remains much traditional *body sense*, especially among rural and working-class women, as well as and in particular religious and ethnic groups, who are more resistant to the fads of modern medicine. The disillusionment of modern middle-class women ought not to be so universally identified with human progress.

It seems to be true that modern living, particularly under suburban conditions, aggravated by the relative isolation of the small modern family, places enormous strain upon the husband-and-wife relation, and thereby on the lives of children. Despite the ideals of romantic love and the postmarital magic of household cleaners and efficient kitchens, the prosaic routines of embodied living persist. The family continues to be woman's work and males continue to leave home for the "wide world" of the factory and office or its mobile equivalent—and many women have both jobs. The consequent discrepancy between the fun culture and the bodily routines of family life means that, if the ideology of happy-go-lucky living is not questioned, males and females alike will experience increasing somatization of their troubles. The displacement of worries into body symptoms can vary from smoking and drinking to drugs, massage parlors, and a whole range of proposed techniques for eroticizing fading marriages. It is to be expected that males and females will react differently to the discrepancy between the embodied reality of the family and its modern ideology of individual happiness and easy living. Educational level and class position, however, also continue to be important variables in how persons manage the reality of family living while striving to save something of its ideology. Thus, working-class mothers may suffer more than middle-class mothers in preserving a traditional family, even though less tempted to challenge its values. Middle-class women often have the best of both worlds, though sometimes they are sure of neither themselves nor their families.[21]

One must, therefore, be extremely cautious in trying to legislate the direction of social change for women and the family, or for any other social group, however damaged, on the basis of the small social science findings to date. Clearly, relevant knowledge will continue to accumulate. We should not forget that our *political education* requires a healthy critical stance towards the fact-finding operations of any social scientist. Many years ago, Lionel Trilling, reviewing Kinsey's *Sexual Behavior in the Human Male*, warned against the bland assumption that the social sciences present us with generalizations that are the staples of a democratic society, which we can resist only at the risk of seeming undemocratic or unprogressive: "We might say that those who most explicitly assert and wish to practice the

democratic virtues have taken it as their assumption that all social facts—with the exception of exclusion and economic hard-
ship—must be *accepted*, not merely in the scientific sense but
also in the social sense, in the same sense, that is, that no judgment must be passed on them, that any conclusion drawn from
them which perceives values and consequences will turn out to
be 'undemocratic.'"[22] Not only is there the trouble that we risk
being considered enemies of democracy if we challenge the assumption that prevailing social trends are necessarily good in
themselves. There is also the difficulty that *what are considered
democratic social trends often merely represent increases in the affluent
options of Western industrial societies.* If we did not hide from ourselves the social costs of many civil rights, we might find that a
number of psychosocial benefits pursued in the West ought to
be postponed in favor of a worldwide program of minimal levels
of nutritional, medical, and public health support.

We know that the world is a kind of body which suffers, as
we do, from misuse. In terms of the world body politic, we are
faced with striking inequalities in access to food, housing, clothing, health, and life expectancy. A relatively small part of the
world monopolizes its resources, suffering from obesity, mental
illness, and boredom, while most of humankind, often in the
service of the over-privileged industrial countries, slaves to gain
a bare existence. Worse still, as new countries enter the path of
economic development, their diets tend to change toward the
consumption of more meat, sugar, eggs, and foods high in ani-
mal-fat content. They simultaneously enter the cycle of coronary heart diseases, diabetes, hypertension, and bowel cancer.
Paradoxically, malnutrition is as associated with overeating as
with the lack of food. In their constant search for basic raw materials the comfortable nations are also able to displace war and
exploitation onto the poorer nations, disrupting their lives even
further. The family of man has a long way to go before it lives
together. A vast number of men, women, and children are still
fighting for:

(1) the right to satisfy their hunger
(2) the right to education

(3) the right to work for a living
(4) the right to be cared for
(5) the right to political organization and freedom of expression.

The terrible thing is that no one's appetite is cut by another's hunger. This is the moral problem facing all industrial societies while they continue to generate incredible differences both between their own members and between themselves and other societies whose economies are weaker. If only a small reduction were made in the world's military capacity for self-destruction, a reasonable floor might be set for the living standard of the world's population.

From all this, we see that one can hardly escape falling back upon the human body as an image for the development of a balanced social and world order. I do not mean that in order to realize such a state we need to reduce humans to a single pattern of living. Moreover, to attain something like *a world right to life*, we cannot do without complex technical and social aid. Nevertheless, what we must avoid is the temptation to attribute any superiority to Western industrial societies over the societies they are currently in a position to help. For in Western societies there is much reason for self-doubt. We are beginning to learn that professionalism and the welfare state are not omnipotent surrogates for the family and the local community. Social science aid in industrial and industrializing societies must increasingly confront the question of how it can work in complementary ways with family and local resources. In fact, there is reason to believe that *we need more than ever to reinvent the family* as a responsible unit of action regarding the welfare of its members in matters of education, consumption, and general health. Here, as so often, progress looks like recycling tradition, even while it requires of us an ever greater critical intelligence.

CHAPTER FIVE

MEDICAL BODIES

IN PRECEDING chapters we have seen how the body politic functions on the economic and political level. It is a complex task to analyze the simultaneous celebration and degradation of the human body in the production, consumption, and administrative processes of modern political economy. What we have observed so far reaches its apogee in the *medicalization* of the body. Here we have a new frontier for industrial societies. Here, above all, is a place for the bureaucratized choreography of professional heroism: one body probing another in the extension of the finest medical technology in the world. No scenario is better suited to modern society: its apparent classlessness, its obvious expertise, and its atheistic humanism are not only the very stuff of medical soap-operas; they are our elemental ideology.

It is beyond the competence of any single scientist to keep abreast of all the developments in medical biology. Indeed, it would be foolish to attempt anything like a rival competence in an area whose experimental literature covers so many subspecialities of the natural sciences while at the same time breaking boundaries with new paradigms of life research. I should also underline that nothing I say is meant to reject what is properly scientific in modern medicine, namely, the way in which it respects nature where nature in fact appears to respect shifting human craft and technological insights into nature's operation, as Jonathan Miller shows so vividly in *The Body in Question*. What a sociologist can offer as a perspective on medical biology is the warning that its discoveries increasingly require us to re-think life, the individual, the family, and society and not simply to accommodate its use as we do with television or the auto-mobile. Even the latter are not easily fitted into the domestic environment without some reshaping and the growth of new dependencies. Hitherto, in a gross way, society has housed the products of the industrial process as we have known it in the last two hundred years. But now we have two new instruments of modern technology capable, at the nuclear end, of destroying human society, while promising, at the medical end, to recreate it. It is this medical promise, and what it holds out for individ-uals, the family, and the modern therapeutic state, that we must examine briefly.

Modern medicine is supremely technocratic and bureau-cratic. Moreover, it is clean. As such it is the envy of all other forms of managerial power in the modern administrative state driven with the dream of therapeutic control. Furthermore, like the state bureaucracy, the medical bureaucracy is self-addicting, with results pointed out by Vicente Navarro:

> Within the last decade the medical establishment has become a major threat to health. The depression, infection, disability, and dysfunction that result from its intervention now cause more suf-fering than all the accidents in traffic and industry. Only the or-ganic damage done by the industrial production of food can rival the ill-health induced by doctors. In addition, medical practice sponsors sickness by the reinforcement of a morbid society which not only industrially preserves its defectives but breeds the thera-pist's client in a cybernetic way. Finally, the so-called health professions have an indirect sickening power, a structurally health-denying effect. They transform pain, illness, and death from a personal challenge into a technical problem and thereby expropriate the potential of people to deal with their condition in an autonomous way.[1]

119

The medicalization of the body is a dramatic part of the pervasive industrialization of the body that we have observed in earlier chapters.[2] Through it we are socialized into bringing every stage of the life cycle—conception, birth, nurturing, sexual conduct, illness, pain, aging, dying—into the administration of bureaucratized centers of professional care which function, in my view, to achieve the defamilization of the body. The ultimate goal of this process, which is accomplished by medicine, psychoanalysis, law and the politics of women's bioliberation, to be specific, is to bring all life into the market place by having its origins and extinction governed by state therapeutic administration. Of course, behind their white coats professional medical bodies hide the same class, sex, and racial characteristics as the wider society from which they appear to be removed: physicians are mostly upper-middle-class white males, nurses and auxiliaries mostly lower-middle or working-class females. Ideologically, the practice of medicine is tied to the mechanistic model, high technology, and a nonsociological approach to health disorders. By the same logic, therapy is individually designed and made compatible with the heavy case loads of monopoly practice through large amounts of chemotherapy, whether imposed or self-administered.

Institutional sources of psychosomatic disorders lie outside the scope of the dominant medical practice. Worker alienation, occupational diseases, and environmental carcinogens, which constitute basic issues in the political economy of medicine, are excluded from the dominant medical model. For example, whereas vast sums of money go for research into heart disease in order to individualize solutions in diet, exercise, and genetic inheritance, the research finding that longevity correlates highly with work satisfaction can be passed over because of its lack of fit with the individualized diagnosis. The report of a special task force to the secretary of Health, Education, and Welfare noted:

In an impressive 15-year study of aging, the strongest predictor of longevity was work satisfaction. The second best predictor was overall "happiness. . . ." Other factors are undoubtedly important—diet, exercise, medical care and genetic inheritance. But research findings suggest that these factors may account for only about 25% of the risk factors in heart disease, the major cause of death. That is, if cholesterol, blood pressure, smoking, glucose level, serum uric acid, and so forth were perfectly controlled, only about one-fourth of coronary heart disease could be controlled. Although research on this problem has not led to conclusive answers, it appears that work role, work conditions, and other social factors may contribute heavily to this "unexplained" 75% of risk factors.[3]

The extent to which the mechanistic model trades upon very definite conceptions of the body, personality, and society for its diagnostic and treatment practices has been nicely summarized by Peter Manning and Horacio Fabrega[4] in a broad comparison of modern impersonalistic medicine and a personalistic folk system:

Self and Body

Impersonal System	Personal System
1. The BODY and the SELF are seen as distinct entities, logically and socially.	1. The BODY and SELF are not seen as logically distinguishable entities: they form a continuum. Changes in one produce and cannot be separated from changes in the other.
2. Health or illness or "normal and sick" may be applied to either the body or the self in a logically consistent fashion.	2. Health and illness cannot be considered logically to be located exclusively in one OR the other entity.
3. SOCIAL RELATIONSHIPS tend to be partitioned, segmented, and situational, i.e., there are many selves and roles which are seen as discontinuous.	3. SOCIAL RELATIONSHIPS tend to be nonpartitioned, diffuse, encompassing, i.e., there are fewer roles and selves and those that do exist are intimately linked.
4. Social relationships are relatively formal and impersonal and are evaluated without a consistent moral-judgmental framework.	4. Social relationships are less formal and more personal and are contained within a consistent moral framework which is legitimated by a higher, i.e., sacred, authority.

121

5. The body is described within a biological framework, i.e., everyday discourse about health concerns is heavily punctuated by the use of biological categories and explanations derived from scientific sources.

6. The body is understood as a complex biological machine.

7. The body's structure and function are partitioned logically into specific parts and systems. The levels of functions and interdependence are differentiated in a relatively precise manner.

8. Health and restoration to health are perceived as dependent on and logically referring to the body as a physical entity or, alternatively, to the self as a mentalistic entity.

9. PERSONALITY is seen as a salient factor in interpersonal relationships—it is the means by which it is believed one shows a "consistent self," and it is conceptualized almost as a distinct entity that explains behavior.

10. CHARACTER TYPES and personality styles are only minimally significant in the diagnosis and treatment of disease. Such labels as "moody," "insensitive," "silly" exist and are socially, not biologically, relevant.

11. DISEASE exists apart from the foregoing modes of self-presentation.

5. The body is not seen as an independent entity separated from interpersonal relations; everyday discourse is low in number of biological terms derived from scientific sources.

6. The body is seen as a wholistic, integrated aspect of self and social relations which is vulnerable and may be easily affected by feelings, other people, natural forces, or spirits.

7. Categories referring to the body are unrefined. The body as an anatomic and physiologic entity is only generally partitioned. A simple view of function, extensions, and meaning of parts is held.

8. Health is equivalent to social equilibrium. In addition to having bodily correlates, restoration to health is seen as a product of (a) reequilibrated or more harmonious social relationships, (b) purging of emotional and spiritualistic forces, and/or (c) restoring equilibrium in socioritualistic bonds.

9. PERSONALITY does not exist as a separate entity; all relationships are transactional and multibonded, and the guiding emotional tone and interpersonal style as revealed in these relationships are what is felt as characteristic of the individual.

10. CHARACTER TYPES and self-presentation are intrinsic or isomorphic to the cause, type, diagnosis, and cure of disease.

11. DISEASE cannot exist apart from these modes of self-presentation.

Ivan Illich has argued that the medicalization of the body in Western industrial societies has reached epidemic levels. This is not, of course, an argument that we can do without medicine. Rather, the question is whether we need *as much* medicine as we have, *for whom* we have it, and *for what* we have it, and whether we should abandon all paramedical and nonmedical practices that have hitherto served to cope with and interpret the ordinary ills of embodied beings. Every day we read about unnecessary surgery, especially for women, excessive dispensing of tranquillizers, and incredibly costly prolongation of life which seems to serve nothing beyond medical technology. Here important factors are the numbers of surgeons, the nature of payment for health services, and the availability of hospital beds and support staff. In exchange for the promise of expertly delivered health, people are induced to bring every stage and facet of life under clinical and hospitalized care. As Illich points out, the medicalization of life is part of its wider industrialization whereby all ordinary human inquiry, curiosity, conflicts, relaxation, leisure, and creativity are increasingly "problematized" in order to bring it under "advice" procedures wherein the expert lawyer, doctor, professor, counsellor, psychiatrist brings lay competences within the orbit of industrial and bureaucratized client relationships: "Medical Nemesis is more than all the clinical iatrogeneses put together, more than the sum of malpractice, negligence, professional callousness, political maldistribution, medically decreed disability and all the consequences of medical trial and error. It is the expropriation of man's coping ability by a maintenance service which keeps him geared up at the service of the industrial system."[5]

The practice of medicine is clearly not examinable apart from the body politic within which it functions and upon which it may have a helpful or an injurious effect. The nature of the intimate bond between medicine and the body politic has been subject to careful comparative study by Richard Titmuss whose arguments, while less flamboyant than those of Illich, nevertheless bear upon the fundamental principles of human community.[6] All the same, Illich's work is important if we understand it to have raised the question of how we should allocate medical resources in a society that daily makes discoveries about the inhumanity of its present market model, ruled more by dealers than healers, as Amitai Etzioni observes. We are living through a biomedical revolution whose aims are typically left to be decided by the professional interests of scientists not responsible for considerating their social and political consequences. It should also be said that inasmuch as the social sciences are themselves enamored of the value-neutral stand of the natural sciences, they are equally unprepared to take in the baby on their doorstep. Any discussion of these issues, therefore, belongs in the public domain. The need for citizens to become involved in examining them represents the greatest challenge to the survival of the body politic. At the same time, it raises crucial problems in political education. Medical biology or biomedicine very soon outstrips the knowledge of all of us whether we have few years of schooling or university degrees, and whether or not we read books, magazines, and newspapers and watch television. We are all ill prepared for the technical details, the complex probability decisions, and the overlapping of engineering and ethical questions that suddenly turn the niceties of affluent medical practice into nightmares of state-administered decisions on life and death.

Biomedicine's technological potential for reshaping the body politic on an individual and a collective level raises some of the most difficult ethical and political decisions facing modern society.[7] Our increasing potential for mechanizing the body politic—for putting it on the machine, so to speak—requires us to make an even greater effort to draw on the moral legacy of the body and its tradition of anthropomorphism if we are to preserve the body politic from total prosthetic dependency. To get a grip on the issues, I want now to follow an argument that reveals how the most profound issues of altruism and self-interest are to be confronted in the choice between market and nonmarket models for the collection and distribution of human blood. With this example clearly in mind, we can then review

the social and political aspects of more esoteric forms of biomedical and genetic engineering.[8] Titmuss writes: "Short of examining humankind itself and the institution of slavery—of men
and women as market commodities—blood as a living tissue
may now constitute in Western societies one of the ultimate
tests of where the 'social' begins and the 'economic' ends. If
blood is considered in theory, in law, and is treated in practice
as a trading commodity then ultimately human hearts, kidneys,
eyes and other organs of the body may also come to be treated
as commodities to be bought and sold in the market place."[9]

In every human community, as in every human being, blood
has always been regarded as the source and symbol of life.
Furthermore, human blood is surrounded with religious awe. It
is the mark of life and death, of health and fertility, of holy sacrifice and unholy murder. Blood is noble when spilled in battle,
ignoble when menstruated. Blood is the vehicle of passion, of
individual and national character. Blood, then, is a cultural object and not only a biomedical object. In short, whatever the
strictly biological problems in thinking the production, compo-
sition, and circulation of blood, we have an equally difficult task
in thinking the social production, consumption, and circulation
of human blood.[10] Of course, it is the efficacy of modern medicine that allows us to deal with the problem at all. But beyond
that, we cannot understand the dimensions of the supply of and
demand for human blood without a knowledge of the social institutions and values which are the equivalent in the body politic of the body's internal blood system. Thus we have to have
some knowledge of the development of medical techniques in
which blood transfusions play a large role—from open heart
surgery and transplants to Caesarian deliveries—as well as the
demand for blood resulting from war, accidents, and the prolongation of life. Within the limits set by matching blood
groups, the perishability of stored blood, the frequency of do-
nations, and the necessary exclusion of certain sectors of the
population (very young, very old, and known disease carriers),
the potential demand for human blood seems to be limited only
by the factors that bear upon the administration and distribu-

tion of its supply. In practice, there will be competition for blood among various medical sectors, giving rise to questions of priority that have to be settled either by relying more or less on market forces or by explicit planning on the lines of socialized medicine. It turns out that in fact the two options are not such clear alternatives, inasmuch as the market model seems to have deleterious effects upon the quality of the blood it collects. Titmuss's evidence shows that the market tends to collect blood from the poor and from captive populations (prisoners, students, military personnel). Often there are problems of donor health, living standards, truthfulness, and the tendency to donate too often to supplement income. Commercial collectors tend to pool blood indiscriminately and to overextend storage limits. The result is a high rate of serum hepatitis and death, particularly among patients over 40, who are principal candidates for blood transfusions. The private market system is dangerous for both recipients and donors.[11] Moreover, it can undermine voluntary donor systems while never being a socially adequate source of supply. Waste through spoilage, unnecessary operations, infectious diseases, and higher mortality rates must also be attributed to the market model, not to mention the social costs of commercializing attitudes toward health and life. Richard Titmuss comments:

> From our study of the private market in blood in the United States we have concluded that the commercialization of blood and donor relationships represses the expression of altruism, erodes the sense of community, lowers scientific standards, limits both personal and professional freedoms, sanctions the making of profits in hospitals and clinical laboratories, legalizes hostility between doctor and patient, subjects critical areas of medicine to the laws of the marketplace, places immense social costs on those least able to bear them—the poor, the sick and the inept—increases the danger of unethical behaviour in various sectors of medical science and practice, and results in situations in which proportionately more and more blood is supplied by the poor, the unskilled, the unemployed, Negroes and other low income groups and categories of exploited populations of high blood yielders. Redistri-

bution in terms of blood and blood products from the poor to the rich appears to be one of the dominant effects of the American blood banking system.[12]

Even in nonethical terms, it turns out that the market model now being advanced for the ever more complex by-products of genetic engineering is economically and administratively, in cost and in quality, inferior to voluntary, altruistic systems of blood supply. Let us, therefore, consider the most recent extensions of biomedicine in order to represent the full extent of the medicalization of the human body and its bearing upon the life of the body politic. Our consideration of the institutional contexts that affect the quality of the blood in our veins—and, as we saw earlier, our food—should be enough to convince us of the intimate ties between society, bodies, and persons which we recollect in the metaphor of the body politic. Consider now how similar considerations bear upon biomedical techniques for intervening in the processes of conception, fertilization, uterine control, delivery, and abortion. At the other end of life, there are technologies for live organ transplants, artificial organs, mechanical extensions of the heart, blood, and kidney systems—if not science fictions of externalized brains. Recently we have been confronted with the growth of embryos *in vitro*, along with fundamental genetic engineering—editing—of DNA material. These experiments are currently viewed as the new market frontier of the biomedical sciences. Initially, the customers are infertile couples, or parents seeking healthy children. Gradually, the market differentiates and the customer looks for preferred timing, gender, and genetic endowment. Before long families, corporations, and governments may place orders for preferred types of human beings or for chemotherapy techniques to modify behavior, moods, and attitudes of individuals to suit institutional needs. The medicalization of the body politic is pushed from both sides—by the consumer family and by the therapeutic state. Thus a huge bioengineering industry can be founded upon the raw materials of human genetics, complete with a banking system for sperm and embryos and an in-

127

ventory of spare parts, to complete the industrialization of the body. Compare the figure of "spare-part man" (Illustration 5) with that of "encyclopedic man" (page 39, above).

The biomedical engineering of the body represents the widening frontier of the industrialization of the body. It is here that the state and the market can exert the deepest influence upon the body politic, forging its genetic material, controlling its demography and social psychology. In this regard, the *prosthetic future* of the human body exists now and is not an imaginary utopia. Paradoxically, the prosthetic possibilities for redesigning the human shape raise in turn the *sociomorphic problem of the kind of society we wish simultaneously to engineer.* It is here that our imagination is more likely to fail us. At the present time, conventional medicine expends incredibly fine skills on the repair of bodies that our society with its present values serves up as war, road, alcoholic, nicotine, coronary, and cancer cases, not to mention the psychosomatic disorders. With existing medical resources, and assuming class differentials in access to public and private medicine, there already arise serious questions regarding medical priorities. These are not easily resolved in terms of cost-benefit analysis, since it is not easy to decide the relative value coefficients of saving lives between young and old persons, employable and unemployable, or between the costs of caring rather than curing, not to mention the difference between social concepts of prevention and delivery and existing medical conceptions of health programs. Moreover, there are crucial problems of law and administration connected with all these issues.

We may ask whether biomedical engineering ought to pursue any and all of its technological possibilities. We may also ask how far society should accord individual rights of access to the potential services of biomedicine. Above all, there are enormously difficult questions concerning the agents of decision in these cases. Should decisions be made by the individual consumer, the family, the doctor, a college of physicians, hospital committees, a community, or medical parliament? Should we run medical lotteries to distribute highly expensive treatments?

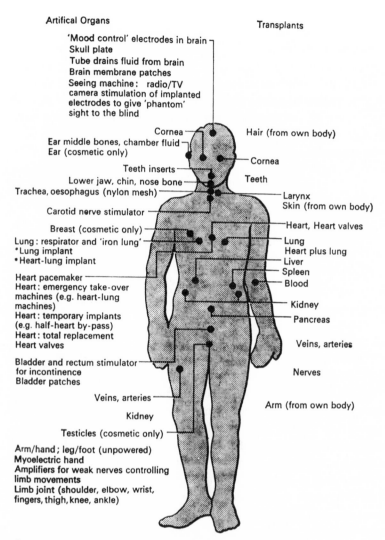

Artifical Organs

'Mood control' electrodes in brain
Skull plate
Tube drains fluid from brain
Brain membrane patches
Seeing machine: radio/TV
camera stimulation of implanted
electrodes to give 'phantom'
sight to the blind

Cornea
Ear middle bones, chamber fluid
Ear (cosmetic only)
Teeth inserts
Lower jaw, chin, nose bone
Trachea, oesophagus (nylon mesh)
Carotid nerve stimulator
Breast (cosmetic only)
Lung: respirator and 'iron lung'
*Lung implant
*Heart-lung implant
Heart pacemaker
Heart: emergency take-over
machines (e.g. heart-lung
machines)
Heart: temporary implants
(e.g. half-heart by-pass)
Heart: total replacement
Heart valves
Bladder and rectum stimulator
for incontinence
Bladder patches
Veins, arteries
Kidney
Testicles (cosmetic only)
Arm/hand; leg/foot (unpowered)
Myoelectric hand
Amplifiers for weak nerves controlling
limb movements
Limb joint (shoulder, elbow, wrist,
fingers, thigh, knee, ankle)

Transplants

Hair (from own body)
Cornea
Teeth
Larynx
Skin (from own body)
Heart, Heart valves
Lung
Heart plus lung
Liver
Spleen
Blood
Kidney
Pancreas
Veins, arteries
Nerves
Arm (from own body)

* = not yet achieved in humans but expected soon

5. Spare-part man. All items other than the lung and heart-lung
implants have been achieved and are expected to have a significant
clinical impact. Trivial artificial parts such as false teeth are not
included; neither are several transplant organs which have been
achieved (whole eye) or are often talked about (limbs from other
bodies, gonads) because of severe technical or ethical difficulties.
Reproduced from Gerald Leach, *The Biocrats* (London: Jonathan Cape;
rpt. Penguin, 1972) by permission of Jonathan Cape Ltd.

The questions are limitless. Do parents have a right to commit embryonic individuals to genetic xeroxing (cloning) in the service of their admiration for entertainers, politicians, sportsmen, and scientists of one kind or another? Should the state intervene to encourage or discourage individual decisions; should it have a biomedical schedule of its own? Some of these options are usefully pictured by Etzioni as follows:[13]

	Therapeutic goals	Breeding goals
Individual service	1. e.g., abort deformed fetuses on demand	3. e.g., artificial insemination; parents' choice of donors features
Societal service *Voluntary*	2. e.g., encourage people to abort a deformed fetus	4. e.g., urge people to use sperm from donors who have high IQs
Coercive	e.g., require a genetic test before marriage license is issued	e.g., prohibit feeble-minded persons from marrying

These choices can be naively conceived as an extension of consumer behavior into sperm shops, embryo banks, abortion clinics, and spare-part warehouses. Indeed, it is possible to imagine some parts of the biomedical apparatus becoming household durables as family members are plugged into various life-support machines for longer or shorter periods. Or rather, such scenarios are conceivable provided we make unexamined assumptions about the relative places of the family, medicine, and the state. One is likely to endorse the growth of biomedicine if one sees it as the servant of ordinary human dilemmas of birth, illness, and untimely death. Once one changes perspective, however, the functions of biomedicine alter. We need to see that there exists a cultural matrix of socialization and individualism which puts a supreme value upon individual life. I deliberately said "individual life" rather than "human life" in order to capture the desperately possessive nature of the concept of individual life. Locked into a rather short biological span, confined to the reduced nuclear family, contemplating childlessness in favour of consumerism, the neo-individual becomes obsessed with the length and physical quality of his or her life. In this concern the medical industry is his or her natural ally. It is there to sell better genetic material, the right child mix, physical, mental and emotional well-being, with a chance of pushing back dying and death into the realm of those brief but remediable technical failures that haunt our more sophisticated machinery.

At the heart of every social system there lies the *reciprocal gift*—the exchange that binds people together for the sake of everything and anything else that they may undertake. Compared with potlatch societies, modern industrial societies may seem weak in this bond. Actually, it is still present; but just as we do not delimit the levels of subsistence and prestige economy, so we tend not to demarcate exchanges in the strictly moral economy. Yet, the medicalization of the body, as Titmuss observes, requires once again that we learn to demarcate an economy of altruism in which we learn once again that we are social bodies.[14] The market is ill prepared to serve the body politic in respect of the new economy of biomedical artifacts, operations, and exchanges. Thus the gift of blood has no price; it must be rich; it cannot be withheld. Its availability is the mark of a charitable society; its collection and distribution articulates the anonymous love of that society's members toward their strangers. The circulation of blood is, therefore, socially speaking just as vital to the life of the ethical community as it is to the life of the individual. Moreover, as Titmuss says, what can be said of blood circulation applies in every detail to the social organization of the more exotic prosthetics of biomedicine:

> The ways in which society organizes and structures its social institutions—and particularly its health and welfare systems—can encourage or discourage the altruistic in man; such systems can foster integration or alienation; they can allow the "theme of the gift" (to recall Mauss's words)—of generosity towards strangers— to spread among and between social groups and generations. This

. . . is an aspect of freedom in the twentieth century which, compared with the emphasis on consumer choice in material acquisitiveness, is insufficiently recognized. It is indeed little understood how modern society, technical, professional, large-scale organized society, allows few opportunities for ordinary people to articulate giving in morally practical terms outside their own network of family and personal relationships.[15]

The medical body is the epitome of consumerism. The biotechnologies that produce and service it represent the last stage in that complex of socioeconomic and political forces that push for the administration of the defamilized individual. The political ideologies of the pill, abortion, and genetic choice tend to gloss over both the biological risks in these emancipatory possibilities and the paradox that these very technologies may well be the agents, via the medicalization of the body, of a system of therapeutic controls that would grip the body politic more firmly than any preceding form of social and political control. What is more, followers of such ideologies are unlikely to see that *social control in liberal welfare states never takes the form of a brave new world when it can trade upon consumerism and welfare rights to recruit individuals for their own subordination.* Marx, however, would not have missed this point, since it was he who first saw that slavery becomes truly historical only when individuals have been defamilized and decommunalized into self-responsible market agents.

With these observations in hand, we may find it easier to understand some of the striking arguments of Michel Foucault,[16] whom critics generally find difficult to follow—very largely because historians and political scientists are not used to seeing the body play such a central role in the analysis of power and scientific discourse. I think, however, that the path we have taken to this point makes it easy to understand Foucault's focus upon *political anatomy.* By stressing that the body is good to *think* and to have, we have laid the ground for Foucault's seemingly complex arguments that power does not function as a possession, or as a force exerted over bodies. The operation of political and economic power does not aim simply to control passive bodies or to restrain the body politic, but *to produce docile bodies.* This means we must set aside views of the political process that derive from a reductive conception of the physical body as pushed by unruly forces that require restraint if moral and political order are to reign in our lives. Once we distinguish the physical body from the communicative body, as we did earlier, it becomes possible to develop autonomous symbolic systems around the physical body—as in art, dance, sport, and, above all, medicine. In turn, medical practice can develop discursive languages designed to externalize, expand, and control health, sexuality, birth, moods, and aggression, for example, well beyond the natural body.

We have seen in earlier chapters how the economy achieves expansion of the productive body. Since power, medicine, and commerce all reach into and expand the productive body, instead of simply creating a passive body, I have argued that we must study the microprocesses of the body politic rather than hang on to ideological formulations of the political superstructure's subordination to the economic infrastructure. Such glosses fail to reveal the overdetermination of the embodied socioeconomic and sociopolitical processes that release individuals into voluntary servitude. Foucault writes in *Discipline and Punish*:

> To analyze the political investment of the body and the microphysics of power presupposes, therefore, that one abandons—where power is concerned—the violence-ideology opposition, the metaphor of property, the model of the contract or of conquest; that—where knowledge is concerned—one abandons the opposition between what is 'interested' and what is 'disinterested', the model of knowledge and the primacy of the subject. Borrowing a word from Petty and his contemporaries, but giving it a different meaning from the one current in the seventeenth century, one might imagine a political 'anatomy'. This would not be the study of the state in terms of a 'body' (with its elements, its resources and its forces), nor would it be the study of the body and its surroundings in terms of a small state. One would be concerned with

133

the 'body politic', as a set of material elements and techniques that serve as weapons, relays, communication routes and supports for the power and knowledge relations that invest human bodies and subjugate them by turning them into objects of knowledge.[17]

What I have tried to show in this and the preceding chapters is that modern society is so thoroughly anthropomorphizing not because of its (obvious) cognitive powers but precisely because the latter are most effective as embodied powers. They rule us by having us rule ourselves as *docile subjects*. Moreover, they are ideologically indifferent—they can as well work through market institutions as the state. In practice, Western societies pursue a certain dependency between the state and the economy which fosters those institutions that erode the bulwark functions of the family and push the individual into the arms of the therapeutic state. No conspiracy is involved here—nor need there be. After all, the economy also sells itself in a therapeutic fashion, affecting to take care of individuals in all of life's contingencies. Businessmen, lawyers, doctors, psychiatrists, and sociologists are, however, able to hide their function as agents of social control from themselves as much as from their clients since they too believe they are either marketing personal services or acting as the agents of rights guaranteed by the state.

It is in this light that we can understand the contemporary therapeutic interest in sexuality, the proliferation of sexual discourse, sexual emancipation, and sexual rights. In *The History of Sexuality* Foucault explains it thus:

> The medical examination, the psychiatric investigation, the pedagogical report, and family controls may have the over-all and apparent objective of saying no to all wayward and unproductive sexualities, but the fact is that they function as mechanisms with a double impetus: *pleasure and power*. The pleasure that comes of exercising a power that questions, monitors, watches, spies, searches out, palpates, brings to light; and on the other hand, the pleasure that kindles at having to evade this power, flee from it, fool it, or travesty it. The power that lets itself be invaded by the pleasure it is pursuing; and opposite it, power asserting itself in

the pleasure of showing off, scandalizing or resisting. Capture and seduction, confrontation and mutual reinforcement: parents and children, adults and adolescents, educator and students, doctors and patients, the psychiatrist with his hysteric and his perverts, all have played this game continually since the nineteenth century. These attractions, these evasions, these circular excitements have traced around bodies and sexes, not boundaries not to be crossed, but *perpetual spirals of power and pleasure.*[18]

In previous chapters we spent considerable time on the symbolic analysis of food and smoking behavior as well as of a number of other bodily techniques. In the chapter on the body politic I suggested that the political process might be formulated in terms of critical discursive strategies designed to analyze and foster values pertinent to the bio-body, the productive body, and the libidinal body as differentiated levels of the family and body politic. Similarly, Foucault proposes four rules for studies of such critical discourse once a given site of power-knowledge— for example the confessional interrogation of "the flesh" or the pedagogical surveillance of the infant body—has been identified:[19]

(I)   *Rule of immanence*

If sexuality was constituted as an area of investigation, this was only because relations of power had established it as a possible object; and conversely, if power was able to take it as a target, this was because techniques of knowledge and procedures of discourse were capable of investing it.

(II) *Rule of continual variance*

We must not look for who has the power in the order of sexuality (men, adults, parents, doctors) and who is deprived of it (women, adolescents, children, patients); nor for who has the right to know and who is forced to remain ignorant. We must seek rather the pattern of modifications which the relationships of force imply by the very nature of their process.

(III) *Rule of double conditioning*

No 'local center', no 'pattern of transformation' could function if, through a series of sequences, it did not eventually enter into an over-all strategy. And, inversely, no strategy could achieve comprehensive effects if it did not gain support from precise and tenuous relations serving, not as its point of application or final outcome, but as its prop and anchor point.

(IV)   *Rule of the tactical polyvalence of discourses*

We must not expect the discourses on sex to tell us, above all, what strategy they derive from, or what moral divisions they accompany, or what ideology—dominant or dominated—they represent; rather we must question them on the two levels of their tactical productivity (what reciprocal effects of power and knowledge they ensure) and their strategical integration (what conjunction and what force relationship make their utilization necessary in a given episode of the various confrontations that occur).

Whatever our propensity to project our own perversity, few people can have failed to notice how much we assault ourselves with sexuality. To some interpreters, this is simply the result of releasing the bonds of law and morality without which sex must overwhelm us. But if we distinguish gendered sex from individualized sexuality, as I argued earlier, then what we are dealing with is an enormous expansion of institutionalized discourse upon sexuality—legal, medical, psychiatric, pedagogic, pornographic—which multiplies the cultural potential of biological sex beyond its intrinsic limits. We then need to ask in whose interest this expansion occurs and by what specific bodily techniques the various discursive strategies are implemented. These questions lead us to the first striking observation. We have increased our control over sex by expanding and releasing a flood of sexualized discourse. The same is true of life. The expansion of scientific discourse about life, genetics, health, subsistence, home conditions, learning abilities, and the like serves to bring life within the orbit of state power and industrialization. Historically, state power was based upon the king's ultimate control over his subjects' bodies—he could commit them to death or grant them continued life. In the modern period, the state in the very name of the therapeutic servicing of its subjects' health fastens more deeply upon their minds and bodies. The two periods represent polar ends in the continuum of biopower:

(1) *An anatomo-politics of the human body*:
     Here power functions as *discipline* and *punishment*. It works through *institutions*—universities, schools, prisons, barracks, factories;
(2) *A biopolitics of the population*:
     Here power functions as the *administration* of the species body—investing in procreation, births, deaths, living standards, physical and mental health. It works through *regulatory controls*.

"Sex" is perfectly suited to be an object of these two strategies of power since they overlap in their operation. On the one hand, "sex" is an object for disciplinary power, while on the other hand sexuality can be psychoanalyzed and medicalized as a discursive strategy of administrative power. Moreover, as I have remarked, these two strategies need not be perfectly in harmony, even though their very conflict betrays a certain pact. Foucault notes:

Whence the importance of the four great lines of attack along which the politics of sex advanced for two centuries. Each one was a way of combining disciplinary techniques with regulative methods. The first two rested on the requirements of regulation, on a whole thematic of the species, descent and collective welfare, in order to obtain results at the level of discipline; the *sexualization of children* was accomplished in the form of a campaign for the health of the race (precocious sexuality was presented from the eighteenth century to the end of the nineteenth as an epidemic menace that risked compromising not only the future health of adults but the future of the entire society and species); *the hysterization of women*, which involved a thorough medicalization of their bodies and their sex, was carried out in the name of the responsibility they owed to the health of their children, the solidity of the family institution, and the safeguarding of society. It was the reverse relationship that applied in the case of *birth controls* and the *psychiatrization of perversions*: here the intervention was regulatory in na-

137

ture but it had to rely on the demand for individual disciplines and constraints (*dressages*). Broadly speaking, at the juncture of the 'body' and the 'population', sex became a crucial target of a power organized around the management of life rather than the menace of death.[20]

It is important to remember that all bodies are *familied bodies*. Thus the strategies of medicalization and psychiatrization have profound implications for the relation between the family and the therapeutic state. Again a two-way strategy is involved. The family is held up as the center for the production of healthy, well-adjusted individuals and at the same time attacked for its abuse of authority, its carelessness and cruelty. The result is that its members are *defamilized* inasmuch as they pursue their rights against the family—divorce, abortion, children's rights—and *family centered* inasmuch as the psychologized family is obliged to valorize its members in preparation for life outside. In short, the family exchanges its traditional authority for its dependency upon a host of therapeutic authorities whose use confers upon the liberalized family the seal of good housekeeping.[21] Such a family totters continuously between falling apart and coming together. Its precariousness is eminently suited to the nondirective intervention of the therapeutic agencies to which the family is obligated. Casting suspicion on the family of origin as a place of injury, the therapeutic complex at the same time reinvents the psychoanalyzed family as an expanding horizon of health and happiness whose only limit is the individual's dependent capacity for therapy.

In making these observtions I am *not* simply lamenting the changing status of the family. An extremely important shift is also involved with respect to our fundamental conceptions of social control and individual responsibility. We are engaged in a significant changeover from a penal to a therapeutic model in dealing with everything from murder, rape, racism, alcoholism, and delinquency to suicide and depression.[22] In the therapeutic model the locus of responsibility for crime or deviance is displaced from the individual to his or her physical, emotional and socioeconomic circumstances. Punishment yields to treatment and therapy. "Illness" and "health" become the discursive strategies for dealing with social problems whether in cities or in individuals. The result is a disinvestment in criminal justice and constitutional law in favor of administrative decisions to cure patients through sterilization, shock therapy, frontal lobotomy, and drug therapy. To be effective the therapeutic strategy ultimately depends upon the realization of the dream of administrative social science—to be able to catalogue and predict antisocial conduct. We cannot pursue all the issues here, though we say something more in the conclusion. What is fundamental is that the American prospects of the therapeutic state have caused its critics to invoke the Ninth Amendment in order to update the defense of the body politic aginst the new therapy. Nicholas Kittrie writes:

> Surely the right to live one's life free from bodily and psychological alteration is basic to our scheme of society. The ability to remain as you are is clearly a right suggested by the general pattern of the Bill of Rights. The First Amendment prohibitions against state invasion of religious freedom and interference with the free transmission of ideas demonstrate that a man's thoughts, mind, conscience, and psychological processes are not to be manipulated or co-erced by the state. Furthermore, the Eighth Amendment indicates that there are limits of human dignity beyond which the state cannot go in defending itself against the most heinous of offenders. Thus, even under a narrow construction of the Ninth Amendment, room can be found for the *right to personality and bodily integrity*.[23]

The prosthetic powers of modern society are very nearly total. Feeding its members into cybernetic, computerized informational, and bureaucratized systems of thought and feeling, modern society has fleshed out machineries of power that threaten community and democracy with extinction. *We are approaching negative anthropomorphism*.. In this there is a huge paradox. Nominally, these developments have occurred in the name of the individual. Indeed, in no other way could the power of the state have so increased—at least in our own society. How is that? A number of factors are now seen to have led in this direction, without our being able to settle narrowly or conspiratorially upon any primary cause. What is important is to discern this social shift and to continue to explore its implications as best we can. The shift has occurred in the modern therapeutic experiment of trying to civilize individuals who have no social commitments to anything but the myth of their own utility. Thus, as Philip Rieff observes: "There is a sense in which culture is always at one with the social system. In a society with so many inducements to self-interest, 'self-realization' seems a noble and healthy end. The least valuable competitive position is to be self-defeating. The therapeutic cannot conceive of an action that is not self-serving, however it may be disguised or transformed. This is a culture in which each views the other, in the fullness of his self-knowledge, as 'trash.'"[24]

For this state of affairs to be achieved, old social commitments—to religion, the family, and community—must be undermined. At the same time, commitment to the lack of commitment must be institutionalized. Therefore, the therapeutic state enters to support the failed families, communities, and psyches that are the cost of *the industrialization of selfishness*, of egoism and materialism. Rieff also remarks: "Quantity has become quality. The answer to all questions of 'what for?' is 'more.' The faith of the rich has always been in themselves. Rendered democratic, this religion presupposes that every man become his own eleemosynary institution. Here is a redefinition of charity from which the inherited faith of Christianity may never recover. Out of this redefinition, Western culture is changing already into a symbol system unprecedented in its plasticity and absorptive capacity. Nothing much can oppose it really, and it welcomes all criticism, for, in a sense, it stands for nothing."[25]

In practice, of course, a system that promotes and relies on individual excess must be surer than ever of individual control. And so we witness the simultaneous extension of economic and state power over the minds and bodies of individuals who are otherwise free to think, feel, and do anything they wish. We have already seen this conbination at work in the activities of consumerism and its biomedical extrapolations. If anything, the psychological man required by the multiplication of needs and desires to be satisfied through science, technology, and the economy is more than ever the mirror-effect of the society he takes to be his reflection. Rieff points out that an unprecedented *narcissistic effect* becomes the controlling and self-committing factor in modern political life:

> All governments will be just, so long as they secure that consoling plentitude of option in which modern satisfaction really consists. In this way the emergent culture could drive the value problem clean out of the social system and, limiting it to a form of philosophical entertainment in lieu of edifying preachment, could successfully conclude the exercise for which politics is the name. Problems of democracy need no longer prove so difficult as they have been. Psychological man is likely to be indifferent to the ancient question of legitimate authority, of sharing in government, so long as the powers that be preserve social order and manage an economy of abundance.[26]

The body politic is not healthy where its life is reduced to the selfish absorption of individuals without a concern for either the collectivity or posterity. The ahistorical consciousness of modern society is a further component in the affinity between secularization and conformity. The loss of a meaningful social or public context for the ideals of individualism, freedom, and equality is reflected in the alienated and confused symbolism in the very titles of David Riesman's *Lonely Crowd* and Paul Goodman's *Growing Up Absurd*. Each of these works confronts us with the paradox that society may be free without individuals being free. The liberal identification of individual and social interests, or, rather, the liberal perception of the challenge and opportunity offered to the individual by society, has withered away into a conviction of the absurdity of society and the idiocy of privatization which is its consequence. For want of a genuine public domain, in which the political and social activities of individuals can achieve a focus and historical perspective, people abandon politics for the civic affirs of suburbia or the "bread and butter" questions of unionism. As individual awareness increasingly shifts toward a concern with consumption, economic knowledge is reduced to a concern with prices in abstraction from the corporate agenda that determines prices. The result is a loss of any coherent ideological awareness of the political and economic contexts of individual action. However, this situation does not represent an end of ideology. It is simply in the nature of the dominant ideology of neo-individualism shaped by the context of corporate capitalism. In order to break the tendency to monetize all individual experience, and in order to shift individual time perspectives away from short-term consumer expectations, it is necessary to institutionalize more universal goals of public, familized, and long-term value. Such a requirement falls outside the pattern of instant satisfactions projected by the consumer orientation. The latter substitutes the thin continuity of progress for the solid accumulation of social history. Any concern with social balance, institutional poverty, and waste or the interaction between politics, economics, nature, and culture presupposes a collective and historical framework. But such a framework is foreign to the liberal ideology of individual agency and its moralistic acceptance of inequality, success, and failure at whatever social cost.

Contemporary discussion of the failure of individualism is largely a lament for the loss of family functions. We view them with nostalgia because the liberation of the individual from the family has not resulted in the emancipation of Eros. To find reasons for this outcome, it has been necessary to rethink the historical functions of the bourgeois family. Their stripping away only released the members of the bourgeois family into the professional, therapeutic, and administrative care of the liberal welfare state.[27] At the same time, the administrative and therapeutic state is ideologically suited to mask the processes of social control that respond to and direct the lives of individuals raised in *families without authority*. In turn, the loss of the bulwark function of the bourgeois family, and the consequent hybridization of the public and private realms into "society," represent the loss of an institutional basis for the role of critical public opinion in the legitimating process of political democracy. With remarkable prescience, Rieff pointed to these trends as the next stage of American culture: "Where family and nation once stood, or Church and Party, there will be hospital and theater too, the normative institutions of the next culture. Trained to be incapable of sustaining sectarian satisfactions, psychological man cannot be susceptible to sectarian control. Religious man was born to be saved; psychological man is born to be pleased. The difference was established long ago when 'I believe,' the cry of the ascetic, lost precedence to 'one feels,' the caveat of the therapeutic. And if the therapeutic is to win out, then surely the psycho-therapist will be his secular spiritual guide."[28]

It remains for us to help to decide whether bourgeois democracy has spent its moral capital to the point where the forces of homogenized administrative culture can no longer be resisted except by fundamentalist and neo-conservative elements. If this is so, then the culture of pathological narcissism, commodity eroticism, and the politics of intimacy represent the narcosis of family authority and authentic individualism. But for thousands of years human society has endured because the family has endured. This is not because we do not suffer in the family. It is because what we learn about suffering and joy in the family within ordinary limits stands by us in the rest of life. Yet in industrial societies we are tempted to destroy the family in the name of the individual—or to push into the ghetto those who remain tied to the family. Today, this trend is more persistent than ever. In its first stages, industrialism moved too fast in shifting the family into the cotton factories, simplifying the machinery enough to be worked by women and children and expelling the men. The men responded by smashing the machines. This reaction horrified the industrialists enough to turn them away from their vision of machines tended by even more degraded creatures such as prisoners, monkeys, and robots. They accepted a stand-off arrangement between the family, the school, and the factory. Some industrialists tried, of course, to

143

substitute paternalism for the familied production of workers. But this attempt could succeed only for a time without becoming too costly economically and politically. In any case, it was a mistaken even if understandable strategy. It wasn't necessary to *produce* the workers who produce everything else. It wasn't necessary even to *own* them in any way that reminded them too obviously of slavery. All that was needed was for industrialism to discover consumerism.

The consumer produces himself and herself provided he and she can be sufficiently defamilized, decommunalized, and rendered déclassé. Everything that weakens the family—not just unemployment but everything that fosters the illusion of individual self-production—strengthens consumerism. In turn, the failures of consumerism—those who do not get enough—strengthen the therapeutic state and its system of emotional transfers. Nowadays, families buy the services of their own children whose rights to pay and parental service are guarded by the threat of malpractice suits. This kind of relationship is not surprising since the contract upon which today's enucleated family is founded is similarly agonistic. If there is any central covenant in such a family, it centers upon a mutual regard for the television wherein such arrangements are commercially celebrated. What is seen is the war of each against all; mothers and fathers stupified by their children; husbands and wives stupified by one another—above all, everyone stupified by their common admiration for commodities. What is more, as the family self-faulted in its capacity to rearrange itself for consumerism, it was aided by the corporate espousal of women's rights and the critique of paternalism on all fronts—except, of course, its own. Stuart Ewen notes:

> As the rise of capitalism had put traditional family life into disarray, it also joined in on the feminist argument that patriarchal society was antiquated and oppressive. . . . Yet while feminism had looked toward a world in which women would appropriate control over their own lives, the corporate debunking of the patriarchy coincided with a general devaluation of all forms of self-

direction. In hailing the *modern woman* as a "home manager" and in celebrating the child as the conscience of the new age, corporate ideologues asserted that each was expected to devote a high degree of obedience to the directives of the consumer market. The industrial elevation of women and children served to relegate the traditional patriarch to an antediluvian, sometimes comic characterization. Here mass culture shared the radical hopes for autonomy and equality. Yet once again, in its depiction of the modern family, the world of mass consumption faltered before the edge of change; as the father of old was relegated to the "dust bin of history," the corporate patriarch was crowned as a just and beneficient authority for a modern age.[29]

In view of the agonistic contract at the center of the consumer family, it is in many ways a spurious question to ask whether the family suffers from the violence that it witnesses on television. Rather, we must understand that the consumer family sees more violence at home than on the street. But what is fundamental is how often this violence is interpreted as a *family affair*, thereby underlining the agonistic contract that is the legal foundation of our society. Where the family cannot deal with its own violence and the results—as though these were aberrations in its ordinary pursuit of passive consumerism—it is obliged to resort to the residual authority figures of the legal and medical apparatus. Thus the therapeutic state acquires a benign face for the distraught family whom it serves and protects. No one notices that in this cycle the authority of the family is reduced by the very process which appears to restore it.

In my view, the subjectivization of political and economic life is the deepest source of the violence that irrupts daily in our society, whether in political assassinations or in the mindless slaughter of unsuspecting people like John Lennon. In these appalling incidents an otherwise insignificant individual is thrust into the collective consciousness of the nation—and even the world. The media solemnly portray a family's loss in a society where the family is brutalized to the lowest point. The further irony is that these null points in our history are always the work of "sick" individuals, without political consciousness and strangers to their own families as much to the society they rage against. Thus the collective evil in the social order is externalized and scapegoated, the criminal and the sacrificial victim each serving to preserve the ideology that individuals are the fundamental social reality. In either case, both destroyer and destroyed are ultimately failed by that huge administrative and therapeutic machine that cultivates the wasteland between the family and political society.

I do not believe that the individual can be sacred or free where society hollows out the family, selling it off to social agencies and otherwise condemning it to consumerism. Today it may be said of the family that life there is "nasty, brutish, and short," as Hobbes once remarked of that state of nature which we now see to be the essential state of modern political economy. Can we live with this? I do not think so. For all we know tells us that human beings are family beings. They are so because they are embodied beings, born from one another and raised by one another. Nothing could be more elemental:

All over the whole round earth and in the settlements, the towns, and the great iron stones of cities, people are drawn inward within their little shells of rooms, and are to be seen in their wondrous and pitiful actions through the surfaces of their lighted windows by thousands, by millions, little golden aquariums, in chairs, reading, setting tables, sewing, playing cards, not talking, talking, laughing inaudibly, mixing drinks, at radio dials, eating, in shirt-sleeves, carefully dressed, courting, teasing, loving, seducing, undressing, leaving the room empty in its empty light, alone and writing a letter urgently, in couples married, in separate chairs, in family parties, in gay parties, preparing for bed, preparing for sleep: and none can care, beyond that room; and none can be cared for, by any beyond that room: and it is small wonder they are drawn together so cowardly close, and small wonder in what dry agony of despair a mother may fasten her talons and her vampire mouth upon the soul of her struggling son and drain him empty, light as a locust shell: and wonder only that an age that has borne its children and must lose and has lost them, and lost life, can bear further living; but so it is. [*Let Us Now Praise Famous Men*][30]

Today history is at a dark noon. Never before has the bond between nature and humankind been so threatened. As I see it, the destructive power unleashed in smashing the atom vastly expanded the breach between ourselves and the first men and women who thought themselves together in their gods and families, who brought nature and themselves into a civil pact that has endured great cycles of history until it fell to us to risk the legacy of mankind in a moment of madness.

THE FUTURE SHAPE
OF HUMAN BEINGS

IN 1982, according to *Time*, the man of the year was a machine. The magazine's cover for January 3, 1983 was devoted to the computer, celebrating that machine's invasion of America. Inside was a story of a second invasion of the American home and heartland, this one by the film *E.T. E.T.* is certainly not a machine, nor a man nor a woman. Like many a man and woman, however, he seems to be a displaced person. Only children—and accompanying adults—understand him, uncertain as both are of their own kind in a world where innocence and friendship are made alien:

Was there a time when dancers with their fiddles
In children's circuses could stay their troubles?
There was a time they could cry over books,
But time has set its maggot on their track
Under the arc of the sky they are unsafe.
What's never known is safest in this life.
Under the skysigns they who have no arms
Have cleanest hands, and, as the heartless ghost
Alone's unhurt, so the blind man sees best.
                                    —Dylan Thomas[1]

148

The computer and E.T. represent two ways of reflecting upon the future shape of human beings—two modes of extraterritoriality that bring into focus the challenge that faces the human imagination in the modern world. If today's humanists are to have any say in the future shaping of human beings, they must take their stand on the alpha and omega questions. They must, in other words, be concerned with the future shaping of life and death—and therefore of the future family. This means, as I have tried to show, that humanists cannot ignore the import of current state and social policy upon the design of life, sexuality, and the family. In short, we are challenged to rethink the human family as the first shape of human beings. With regard to these questions, we stand in a landscape as wild as that in which Vico's first men once stood, listening for the lightning sounds from which they shaped the world's earliest poem, thereby giving to their awkward bodies the human shape of familied society:

> Of such natures must have been the first founders of gentile humanity when at last the sky fearfully rolled with thunder and flashed with lightning, as could not but follow from the bursting upon the air for the first time of an impression so violent. . . . Thereupon a few giants, who must have been the most robust, and who were dispersed through the forests on the mountain heights where the strongest beasts have their dens, were frightened and astonished by the great effect whose cause they did not know, and raised their eyes and became aware of the sky. And because in such a case the nature of the human mind leads it to attribute its own nature to the effect, and because in that state their nature was that of men all robust bodily strength, who expressed their very violent passions by shouting and grumbling, they pictured the sky to themselves as a great animated body, which in that aspect they called Jove, the first god of the so-called greater gentes, who meant to tell them something by the hiss of his bolts and the clap of his thunder. And thus they began to exercise that natural curiosity which is the daughter of ignorance and the mother of knowledge, and which, opening the mind of man, gives birth to wonder.[2]

Vico's *New Science* teaches us that radical anthropomorphism is the creative spring of our humanity. It is a conceit of rationalism that the human spirit can be dominant long after it has suppressed its origins in poetry. We cannot sufficiently stress the originality of our forefathers, those giants (*grossi bestioni*) upon whose poetry is founded the entire rationalist tradition. Whatever their ingenuity, all later thinkers stand in a necessary historical line from the first men whose awkward bodies ruled them as the generative source of our metaphors, relationships, concepts, and generalizations. This is the historical ground of common sense considered as an achievement that is fundamental to any higher unity of humankind. Radical humanism, therefore, cannot be forgetful of its origins without risking its very future. We stand upon the shoulders of those giants who first gave the thundering sky a great body like their own and who made Jove their god, ruler of all men, source of all things. Gathered under Jove's saving rule, our giants thereby established the first human communities—under vulgar law, religiously, and without the conceits of rationalist philosophy. Therefore, our humanity owes itself to those first giant bodies who scared themselves into being ruled by their own fantastic ideas of frightful religions, terrible paternal powers, and sacred ablutions. To these awkward ancestors we owe the foundations of our education, ruling us in ourselves, in our minds and bodies, and in our households:

> The heroes apprehended with human senses those two truths which make up the whole of economic doctrine, and which were preserved in the two Latin verbs *educere* and *educare*. . . .the first of these applies to the education of the spirit and the second to that of the body. The first, by a learned metaphor, was transferred by the natural philosophers to the bringing forth of forms from matter. For heroic education began to bring forth in a certain way the form of the human soul which had been completely submerged in the huge bodies of the giants, and began likewise to bring forth the form of the human body itself in its just dimensions from the disproportionate giant bodies.[3]

All later humanity is indebted to the vulgar metaphysics of the first incorporation whereby our giant ancestors proportioned themselves to the human frame, educating their bodies to suit them to the basic institutions of civil humanity—to religion, marriage, and burial. The power of the *New Science* lies in the calm with which it measures and recovers the distance between science and poetry as fundamental modifications of the human mind and senses. For this reason Vico's giants are neither figments of sentimentalized imagination nor fictions of an objective science of history. Rather, they are the natural agents of a history that is made intelligible through our effort to read and hear it as the history of our own anthropomorphosis:

> From these first men, stupid, insensate, and horrible beasts, all the philosophers and philologians should have begun their investigations of the wisdom of the ancient gentiles; that is, from the giants in the proper sense in which we have just taken them. . . . And they should have begun with metaphysics, which seeks its proofs not in the external world but within the modifications of the mind of him who meditates it. For since this world of nations has certainly been made by men, it is within these modifications that its principles should have been sought.[4]

Just as the first men were called upon to think the world with their bodies, today we must once again rethink society and history with our bodies. We must do so in order to restore the lost shape of our humanity which we portray to ourselves in robots, mummies, and E.T. dolls while pretending a civilized distance between early men and ourselves. We must learn like Vico's giants how to "phone home." Therefore, I want now to propose the following construct, a piece of historical ricolage that may seem even more crude than E.T.'s desperate device. I want to join the embodied history of the first humans to the disembodied history of today's world. I wish to join the first appearance of our humanity to the present disappearance of our own kind as we may see it in passages I shall take from *Time*, the sociologist's poor Homer. The anthropomorphic history that I have recovered from Vico, I shall call *history as biotext*—having in mind the creativity of the impulse to give to history and society a living human shape. The history to which I now turn I shall call *history as sociotext*. Here what I have in mind is the complex of human sciences designed to rewrite the human body, to reinscribe its mind and emotions. We have been concerned with these two histories throughout this book. I do not consider the shift from biotext to sociotext has been motivated by any antihumanist conspiracy. *Nihil Americanum me alienum puto*. Rather, it is our task as radical humanists to consider our extraterritorial designs upon ourselves as the next stage of anthropomorphism. Nor is this to recommend fatalism. We must analyze, evaluate, foster what benefits and resist whatever tendencies we consider threatening to our own kind.

Our situation, as we have considered it in the previous chapter, requires us to think of all technology as biotechnology—to see, in other words, that *every power over nature is a power over ourselves*. Such power is not only present in our machines but proliferates in the discursive production of the human sciences designed to control life, thought, health, sanity, and knowledge. An escalation of this power occurs once the modern therapeutic state discovers that the will to knowledge can be conscripted to redesign the beginnings and ends of life and to administer its course as a *sociotext*.[5] Of course, society has always shaped life, as I have tried to show throughout this work, But we appear now to stand on a frontier where the origins and ends of life converge, making us more of a question for ourselves than ever before. To follow the shift from biotext to sociotext, we need to bring attention to the significance of the modern spectacle of life and death, once a theater of cruelty and now a smooth medicalized scenario, glimpses of which are brought to us through television and the print media. The modern therapeutic state aims, as I see it, to rewrite the biotext as sociotext, binding everybody into a new Leviathan. Thus the state is now concerned to legislate the origins and ends of life, to contracept and to abort, to marry, separate, and divorce, to declare sane and insane, to incarcerate, and to terminate life. Increasingly, the therapeutic state also seduces us into conformity through our desire for health, education, and employment—not to mention happiness, at least as an American aspiration.

This complex of ideas is what I have in mind when I say all our technologies are biotechnologies and that, in turn, they are all strategies for shifting from the primary biotext to a sociotext in which the human shape of human beings is being recast. This shift can, of course, be in the direction of humanitarian goals: the release of individualism, the rights of women and children, and the end of families. From this perspective, we seek to avoid genetic and social damage, and we may even wish to improve our biological legacy. Our motives in pursuing these ends are undoubtedly humane. Yet our experimental technologies for deriving our humanity from laboratory animals and our genetic materials may in practice be inhumane. Indeed, enormous concern already exists on this score and considerable legislative activity is going on, which I cannot possibly describe here.[6] In this regard, however, the life of science, and not only of the life sciences, is sure to be invoked as the highest conception we have of ourselves. This view is likely to prevail, I think, because we now conceive of life itself as the very elemental structure of communication (the DNA code) into which all other discursive codes can be channeled in order to amplify the expression of life. Gerald Leach writes:

> To see what is involved, one has to start by looking at the raw material the aspiring gene surgeon has to work on. *His ultimate task is to edit the master tapes of life*—the wispy, thread-like molecules of DNA in every cell which carries the *hereditary message*— and to edit them so precisely and controllably that a single defective gene here or there can be snipped out or replaced by a normal one . . . he has a tricky job to do. It has been compared to altering a single letter in a copy of the Bible which cannot be opened and has been shrunk to the size of a pinhead. To make things worse, one might add that no one has read more than a paragraph or two of *the hereditary Bible*.[7]

Biotechnology must currently be seen in terms of two prosthetic strategies, one now largely available, and the other increasingly possible. I refer to (1) *spare-part prosthetics* and (2) *genetic prosthetics*. We might think of these as two strategies to shift us from the design of spare-part man to the invention of *prosthetic man*.[8] Although seemingly on the same biomedical frontier, the two projects are in fact as far apart as the stages of early and late capitalism. That is to say, the economy of spare-part prosthetics involves us in a combination of medical craft and commercial banking and distribution procedures. Such systems may be entrepreneurially or state managed, and both may draw upon voluntary donors. As we saw earlier, Titmuss has shown that in the case of blood a number of problems with quality and continuity arise when the spare-part supply depends on commercial rather than voluntary services. In the long run the problems of the spare-part economy may be circumvented whenever it becomes possible to anticipate genetic faults and to correct them at the DNA level. To the extent that such genetic engineering is possible—and its potential should not be exaggerated—we might then implant the basic market rationality of efficiency and choice at the very DNA level. Thus we might contemplate parental choice of biologically perfect embryos. A mark of such perfection, from the point of view of parents, would consist in the embryonic replication (cloning) of themselves or of their social idols. If ever these possibilities emerge, then biotechnology will finally deliver the myth of Narcissus from its mirror. As I see it, it will defamilize the body and the imagination of future individuals, making them the creatures of the dominant ethos of the *market or the state as matrix*. Under such conditions, the institution of life, and not only its bioconstitution, will be radically altered. Our religious and political institutions, the Bible and Parliament, will cease to be our originary institutions. In the laboratory and the clinic, life no longer has any history. Birth will become a consumer fiction, like Mother's Day. Thereafter our hitherto embodied and familied histories will float in a commercial narcosis monopolized by an entrepreneurial or statist biocracy.

I turn now to life at the other end. Despite contemporary atrocities, we consider that in the West we have progressively made death more "humane." The gallows, the guillotine, the gas chamber, the electric chair have all been considered stages in the humanity of death by execution. In December 1982, a new height was reached when a lethal injection of a mixture of sodium thiopental, pancuronium bromide, and potassium chloride was administered to Charles Brooks in a Texas prison. *Time* noted that there was "nothing new" in Brook's medicalized execution, since Socrates seems to have had first claim to hemlock. The appeal to efficiency and reasonableness of punishment has a long history in the enlightened human sciences. The medicalization of the practice of execution appears thus to be the last stage in the humanity of death. It permits us to believe that the disciplinary and punitive order required by our collective life might be exercised as an act of individual love and subjectivized care. To date, medicalized executions are not a general practice. However, should the death penalty be restored, one can expect this rationale for them to be invoked. We can expect it because medicalization is a general feature in the practice of managing deviants, insane, clinically hospitalized, and imprisoned populations. Pharmacological therapies are widespread practices both inside and outside these institutions. Self-administered drugs—the so-called nonmedical uses—are part of the same complex whereby individuals are treated, or treat themselves, as the troubled agents of society. Indeed, the tranquilizing of citizens is the most distinctive feature of the modern therapeutic state. It is the hallmark of our medicalized humanity.[9] From birth to death, from school, work, prison, and play, we can expect to be drugged in order to preserve the dream of secularized happiness in a world unable to deliver its reality.

Psychotropically induced tranquility is a marvelous irony of modern life. It bespeaks the determination to be in control while out of control, to be calm in a state of crisis. Drug use makes the mind the prison of the body in a terrible reversal of the terms of ancient morality. The intervening mechanism is the creation of a society that claims to dominate nature while so many of its members are powerless and out of touch with their own nature. Thus the great natural events of birth, labor, marriage, and death are removed from our humanity in the name of our industrialized society, which experiences its liturgical moments as medicalized, pharmacological events tied to the professional practice of administered care.

In the same issue of *Time* that reported Charles Brooks's medicalized death (December 20, 1982), there is the story of Barney Clark's experience with the implantation of an artificial heart, Jarvik-7, an event marred only by his home having been vandalized in his absence. Here we have the heroic end of medicine extending life—or death—for 112 days, displacing malfunctioning organs. The social and ideological investment in the success of these practices is huge, and overdetermines the drama of intimate fates. The Barney Clark story (pp. 52–55) is immediately followed by an account of genetic "surgery" employing recombinant-DNA techniques to replace "bad" genes with "good" in order to improve the quality of life. The Show Business section carries the story of *Tootsie*—1982's most celebrated anthropomorphosis. In this film an unsuccessful male actor, Michael Dorsey, finds success as Dorothy Michaels, coming to the (offstage?) conclusion: "I was a better man as a woman with a woman than I've been as a man with a woman." Here, of course, there are huge issues that transcend the biological manipulation of life, affecting the very core of our will-to-produce the family as a man-and-woman-shaping institution. In the Behavior Section we then find a report called "The Hollowing of America," in which the crippling affects of narcissism upon the family, school, and workplace are deplored. It would seem that none of these issues should escape our attention and that somehow they challenge us to bring them into focus in the light either of our sense of basic values, which might deplore them, or else of some more profound grasp of the future shape of human beings of which they are the portent. But, sadly, *Time* has no time to construct the interpretive framework of historical and structural analysis that I have required of the reader to this point.

Time, then, destroys our memory by keeping us up to date, just as it defamilizes us by keeping us in touch with the world viewed from America. In it we encounter the difference between the embodied time and family of common-sense knowledge and the tempo of information that makes us obeselescent the more we are addicted to it. If social scientists have a Homer or Virgil, it cannot by now be much more than their daily readings of the press and television. In keeping with such practice, I have culled from *Time* a sample of events that reveal how the human shaping of human beings is a feature of our everyday lives and not an utterly remote utopia of morality and medicine, and perhaps no less strange than the practices of our giant ancestors told in Vico's *New Science*. In conclusion, I shall keep within the philosophical limits of the *Time* 'Essay'—'Do Not Go Gentle Into That Good Night'. In a remarkable page, Roger Rosenblatt muses on the irony of the medical inventiveness employed in the cases of Brooks and Clark, one to die, the other to live. He is rightly puzzled by the civilizing intentions behind each operation, unable to balance the hope in one case against the despair in the other. What obsesses him is the removal of the executioner's deed from visibility. Even though there was a death watch for Charlie Brooks, the medical execution did not show itself; it did not write itself upon the body as our own deed. Here the sociotext erases any trace of the biotext, putting the administration of Brooks's death beyond our humanity. Rosenblatt appears to be pleading for a public death, for a restoration of the theater of life and death in which we can be restored to the sense of our own good and evil. Unlike the Cross or the Star of David, the photos and magazine sketches that trace Brooks's death in the pages of *Time* leave us with no acceptable icon of human suffering. The medical sleep erases the epiphany of death and our remembrance of life. Here, then, with the poet we must cry:

> Do not go gentle into that good night
> Old age should burn and rave at close of day
> Rage, rage against the dying of the light.

> Though wise men at their end know dark is right,
> Because their words had forked no lightning they
> Do not go gentle into that good night.

Good men, the last wave by, crying how bright
Their frail deeds might have danced in a green bay,
Do not go gentle into that good night.

Wild men who caught and sang the sun in flight,
And learn, too late, they grieved it on his way,
Do not go gentle into that good night.

—Dylan Thomas[10]

Today, we are threatened with the prospect of an eternal darkness that may burst upon us from those burning suns we toy with turning against ourselves. Truly, we are living in a dry season, unsure that anything will take root, sap, and bloom; and cannot tell our children otherwise, nor any god.

NOTES

PREFACE   The Prosthetic God

1. Sigmund Freud, *Civilization and Its Discontents*, tr. and ed. James Strachey (New York: Norton, 1962), pp. 38–39. Here it is a pleasure to recognize several years' conversation with my colleague Kenneth Morrison, who has always shaped my ideas, and to thank him for constant borrowings from his Freud collection in the past year. And, as ever, Tom Wilson.

INTRODUCTION   Our Two Bodies

1. See my *Perception, Expression and History* (Evanston: Northwestern University Press, 1970), chap. 4, "Corporeality and Intersubjectivity."

2. Maurice Merleau-Ponty, *Phenomenology of Perception*, tr. Colin Smith (London: Routledge & Kegan Paul, 1962), p. 146.

3. See Marjorie Grene, *Approaches to Philosophical Biology* (New York: Basic, 1965).

4. Here is the occasion to thank several generations of students at York University who suffered incarceration in Sociology 397.6, and, most of all, my teaching assistant, Barbara Petrocci.

5. See Marcel Mauss, "Techniques of the Body," *Economy and Society*, 2 (1973), 70–88.

6. Michel Foucault, *The History of Sexuality*, Vol. I: *An Introduction*, tr. Robert Hurley (New York: Vintage, 1980), p. 103.

7. See Ivan Illich, *Gender* (New York: Pantheon, 1982).

8. See my "Defamilization and the Feminization of Law in Early and Late Capitalism," *International Journal of Law and Psychiatry*, 5 (1982): 255–269.

9. Gertrude Stein, *The Making of Americans* (New York: Harcourt Brace, 1934), p. 128.

10. John O'Neill, *Sociology as a Skin Trade: Essays towards a Reflexive Sociology* (New York: Harper & Row, 1972), p. 10.

11. See my "On Simmel's 'Sociological Apriorities,'" *Phenomenological Sociology: Issues and Applications*, ed. George Psathas (New York: Wiley, 1973), pp. 91–106.

12. See my "Authority, Knowledge and the Body Politic," in *Sociology as a Skin Trade*, pp. 68–80.

13. Merleau-Ponty, *Phenomenology of Perception*, p. 167.

14. Charles Horton Cooley, *Human Nature and the Social Order*. (New York: Schocken, 1964), pp. 183–185.

15. See my "Embodiment and Child Development: A Phenomenological Approach," pp. 65–81, in Hans Peter Dreitzel, ed., *Recent Sociology No. 5: Childhood and Socialization* (New York: Macmillan, 1973); reprinted in *The Sociology of Childhood: Essential Readings*, ed. Chris Jenks (London: Batsford, 1982), p. 76–86.

16. Pierre Bourdieu, "Remarques provisoires sur la perception sociale du corps," *Actes de la Recherche en Sciences Sociales*, April 14, 1977, pp. 51–54.

17. See my "Lecture visuelle de l'espace urbain," *Colloque d'esthétique appliquée à la création du paysage urbain: Collection presenté par Michel Conan* (Paris: Copedith, 1975), pp. 235–247.

CHAPTER ONE   The World's Body

1. For a critique of abstract sociological principles and a defense of radical anthropomorphism see my *Making Sense Together: An Introduction to Wild Sociology* (New York: Harper & Row, 1974).

2. See Leonard Barkan, *Nature's Work of Art; The Human Body as Image of the World* (New Haven: Yale University Press, 1975); and George Perrigo Conger, *Theories of Macrocosms and Microcosms* (New York: Columbia University Press, 1922).

3. *The New Science of Giambattista Vico*, tr. from the Third Edition by Thomas Goddard Bergin and Max Harold Fisch (Ithaca: Cornell Uni-

versity Press, 1970), paras. 236–237. See also my "Time's Body: Vico on the Love of Language and Institution," in *Giambattista Vico's Science of Humanity*, ed. Giorgio Tagliacozzo and Donald Phillip Verene (Baltimore: Johns Hopkins University Press, 1976), pp. 333–339.

4. Emile Durkheim and Marcel Mauss, *Primitive Classification*, tr. and ed. with an introduction by Rodney Needham (London: Cohen & West, 1963), pp. 82–83.

5. Vico, *The New Science*, para. 405.

6. Geneviève Calame-Griaule, *Ethnologie et langage: La parole chez les Dogon* (Paris: Gallimard, 1965), p. 27; Victor Turner, "The Word of the Dogon," in his *Dramas, Fields, and Metaphors: Symbolic Action in Human Society* (Ithaca: Cornell University Press, 1974), pp. 156–165.

7. Marcel Griaule, *Conversations with Ogotommêli: An Introduction to Dogon Religious Ideas* (London: Oxford University Press, 1965); in future cited as *Ogotemmêli*. The following account is, of course, only a paraphrase of a few of the conversations. I am also aware that Anglo-American and French ethnographers have quite different approaches to the Dogon. See Turner, "The Word of the Dogon"; and Mary Douglas, "If the Dogon . . .", in her *Implicit Meanings: Essays in Anthropology* (London: Routledge & Kegan Paul, 1975), pp. 124–141.

8. *Ogotemmêli*, p. 28.

9. *Ogotemmêli*, p. 29.

10. *Ogotemmêli*, p. 39.

11. *Ogotemmêli*, p. 39.

12. Calami-Griaule, *Ethnologie et langage*, pt. I, chap. v; pt. IV, chap. 1.

13. Jean-Paul Lebeuf, *L'habitation des Fali: Montagnards du Cameroun septentrional* (Paris: Hachette, 1961).

14. *Plato's Cosmology: The "Timaeus" of Plato*, tr., with commentary, by Francis MacDonald Cornford (New York: Liberal Arts Press, 1957), 32c–33b, p. 52.

15. Barkan, *Nature's Work of Art*, p. 24.

16. On the rivalry between anthropomorphic and allegorical interpretations of the Bible see A. Marmorstein, *The Old Rabbinic Doctrine of God, II. Essays in Anthropomorphism* (Oxford: Oxford University Press, 1937).

17. Barkan, *Nature's Work of Art*, p. 28.

18. Thomas R. Frosch, *The Awakening of Albion: The Renovation of the Body in the Poetry of William Blake* (Ithaca: Cornell University Press, 1974).

19. *The Complete Prose and Poetry of William Blake,* newly revised edition, ed. David V. Erdman (Berkeley: University of California Press, 1982), p. 257.

20. Mircea Eliade, *The Forge and the Crucible: The Origins and Structures of Alchemy,* tr. Stephen Corrin. 2d ed. (Chicago: University of Chicago Press, 1978, pp. 34–42.

21. Otto Rank, *Art and Artist: Creative Urge and Personality Development,* tr. Charles Francis Atkinson (New York: Agathon Press, 1968), pp. 134–135.

22. Claude Lévi-Strauss, *The Savage Mind* (Chicago: University of Chicago Press, 1966).

23. Lévi-Strauss, *Savage Mind,* p. 16.

24. See Morris Berman, *The Reenchantment of the World* (Ithaca: Cornell University Press, 1981).

CHAPTER TWO   Social Bodies

1. Lévi-Strauss, *Savage Mind,* pp. 168–169.

2. For an elegant introduction to the various dimensions of body metaphors in social thought, see Donald G. MacRae, "The Body and Social Metaphor", in *The Body as a Medium of Expression: An Anthology,* ed. with an introduction by Jonathan Benthall and Ted Polhemus (New York: Dutton, 1975), pp. 59–73.

3. Robert Hertz, *Death and the Right Hand,* tr. Rodney and Claudia Needham (Glencoe, Ill.: Free Press, 1960).

4. Hertz, *Death and the Right Hand,* p. 98.

5. Mary Douglas, *Purity and Danger: An Analysis of Concepts of Pollution and Taboo* (Harmondsworth: Penguin, 1970); *Natural Symbols: Explorations in Cosmology* (Harmondsworth: Penguin, 1973); *Implicit Meanings; Essays in Anthropology* (London: Routledge & Kegan Paul, 1975); and "Cultural Bias" (London: Royal Anthropological Institute of Great Britain and Ireland, Occasional Paper no. 35, 1978). Professor Douglas was kind enough to make extensive critical comments on an early version of my work. I fear she may feel that her efforts to warn me away from the romance of bodies were wasted upon an inveterate millenarian. For all that, her work is important to my thought.

6. Douglas, *Purity and Danger,* p. 48.

7. Jean Soler, "The Dietary Prohibitions of the Hebrews," *The New York Review of Books,* June 14, 1979, pp. 24–30. See also Edmund R.

Leach, "Genesis as Myth," in *Myth and Cosmos: Readings in Mythology and Symbolism*, ed. John Middleton (Garden City, N.Y.: Natural History Press, 1967), pp. 1–13.

8. Soler, "Dietary Prohibitions," p. 30.

9. Ralph Bulmer, "Why Is the Cassowary not a Bird? A Problem of Zoological Taxonomy among the Karam of the New Guinea Highlands," *Man*, n.s. 2 (March 1967), 5–25; S. J. Tambiah, "Animals Are Good to Think and Good to Prohibit," *Ethnology*, 8 (October 1969), 424–459. Both these articles are easily available in Mary Douglas, ed., *Rules and Meanings: The Anthropology of Everyday Knowledge* (Harmondsworth: Penguin, 1973).

10. See Durkheim and Mauss, *Primitive Classification*.

11. Mary Douglas, "Deciphering a Meal," in her *Implicit Meanings*, p. 272.

12. Marvin Harris, "Pig Lovers and Pig Haters," in his *Cows, Pigs, Wars and Witches: The Riddles of Culture* (London: Fontana, 1977), pp. 31–186; also "Forbidden Flesh," in his *Cannibals and Kings* (London: Fontana, 1978), pp. 142–154. See also Marshall Sahlins, "Culture as Protein and Profit," *The New York Review of Books*, November 23, 1978, pp. 45–53; "Cannibalism: An Exchange," *The New York Review of Books*, March 22, 1979, pp. 45–47; Marvin Harris, "Cannibals and Kings: An Exchange," *The New York Review of Books*, June 28, 1979, pp. 51–53. Finally, anyone interested in the status of this controversy must read, along with the comments and Harris's reply, a superb essay by Paul Diener and Eugene E. Robkin, "Ecology, Evolution, and the Search for Cultural Origins: The Question of Islamic Pig Production," *Current Anthropology*, 19 (September 1978), 493–540.

13. Harris, *Cannibals and Kings*, pp. 203–204.

14. B. A. Baldwin, "Behavioral Thermoregulation," in *Heat Loss from Animals and Man: Assessment and Control*, ed. J. I. Monteith and L. E. Mount (London: Butterworth, 1974), pp. 97–117.

15. On this, see Mary Douglas, "The Bog Irish," in her *Natural Symbols*, pp. 59–76.

16. Harris, *Cannibals and Kings*, p. 154.

17. See Marshall Sahlins, *Culture and Practical Reason* (Chicago: University of Chicago Press, 1976); Edmund Leach, *Claude Lévi-Strauss* (New York, 1970); Claude Lévi-Strauss, *The Raw and the Cooked: Introduction to a Science of Mythology*, Vol. 1, tr. John and Doreen Weightman (New York: Harper & Row, 1970); also his "Le triangle culinaire," *L'Arc*, no. 26 (1965), pp. 19–29.

18. Sahlins, "Food Preference and Tabu in American Domestic Animals," followed by "Notes on the American Clothing System," in his *Culture and Practical Reason*, pp. 170–204.

19. Edmund Leach, "Anthropological Aspects of Language: Animal Categories and Verbal Abuse," in *New Directions in the Study of Language*, ed. Eric H. Lenneberg (Cambridge: MIT Press, 1964), pp. 23–63. Actually, Leach's thesis is more refined than the one present here. He is concerned with the link between degrees of sexual access and animal categories in order to explain the latter's role in verbal abuse.

20. See M. A. Crawford and J. P. W. Rivers, "The Protein Myth," in *The Man/Food Equation*, Ed. F. Steele and A. Bourne (New York: Academic Press: 1975), pp. 235–245.

21. Georg Borgstrom, *The Food and People Dilemma* (Belmont, Calif.: Duxbury Press, 1973, p. 64.

22. Frances Moore Lappé, *Diet for a Small Planet* (New York: Ballantine, 1975), pp. 13–14.

23. Alexander Cockburn, "Gastro-Porn," *The New York Review of Books*, December 8, 1977, pp. 15–19.

CHAPTER THREE The Body Politic

1. Barkan, *Nature's Work of Art*, p. 62.

2. *The Republic of Plato*, Bk II, II372A–374E.

3. Livy, *The Early History of Rome*, Books I–IV of *The History of Rome from Its Foundation*. Tr. Aubrey de Selincourt (Harmondsworth: Penguin, 1960), pp. 141–142.

4. See John A.T. Robinson, *The Body: A Study in Pauline Theology* (London: SCM Press, 1952).

5. Ernst Kantorowicz, *The King's Two Bodies* (Princeton: Princeton University Press, 1957), p. 13.

6. Kantorowicz, *King's Two Bodies*, p. 201.

7. Paul Archambault, "The Analogy of the 'Body' in Renaissance Political Literature," *Bibliothèque d'Humanisme et Renaissance*, 29 (1967), 21–63.

8. Sir John Fortescue, *De laudibus legum Angliae*, ed. and tr. with introduction and notes by S. B. Chrimes (Cambridge: Cambridge University Press, 1942), p. 31.

9. *The Complete Essays of Montaigne*, tr. Donald M. Frame (Stanford: Stanford University Press, 1965), Bk. III: 9:732–733. See also Carol E.

Clark, "Montaigne and the Imagery of Political Discourse in Sixteenth Century France," *French Studies*, 24, (October 1970): 337–355.

10. *The Discourses of Niccolo Machiavelli*. Tr. with an introduction and notes by Leslie J. Walker (London: Routledge & Kegan Paul, 1950), Bk III, Discourse 10.

11. *De laudibus legum Angliae*, p. 33.

12. See Otto Gierke, *Political Theories of the Middle Age*, tr. with an introduction by F. W. Maitland (Cambridge: University Press, 1958), pp. 67–73.

13. See Jürgen Habermas, *Legitimation Crisis*, tr. Thomas McCarthy (Boston: Beacon, 1975).

14. Habermas, *Legitimation Crisis*, pp. 36–37.

15. Jean Bethke Elshtain, *Public Man, Private Woman: Women in Social and Political Thought* (Oxford: Martin Robertson, 1981), p. 333.

16. See my "Defamilization and the Feminization of Law in Early and Late Capitalism."

17. Richard Busaca and Mary P. Ryan, "Beyond the Family Crisis," *Democracy*, 2 (Fall 1982), 79–92; compare also Andrew Hacker, "Farewell to the Family?" *The New York Review of Books*, March 18, 1982, pp. 37–44.

18. Christopher Lasch, "Life in the Therapeutic State," *The New York Review of Books*, June 12, 1980, pp. 24–32.

19. Stuart Ewen, *Captains of Consciousness: Advertising and the Social Roots of the Consumer Culture* (New York: McGraw-Hill, 1976), p. 184.

20. See my "Looking into the Media: Revelation and Subversion," in *Communication Philosophy and the Technological Age*, ed. Michael J. Hyde (University: University of Alabama Press, 1982), p. 73–97.

21. See Burton J. Bledstein, *The Culture of Professionalism: The Middle Class and the Development of Higher Education in America* (New York: Norton, 1978).

22. Jacques Donzelot, *The Policing of Families*, tr. Robert Hurley (New York: Pantheon, 1979), p. 94.

23. See Julia Brophy and Carol Smart, "From Disregard to Disrepute: The Position of Women in Family Law," *Feminist Review*, 9 (1981), 3–15; Mary McIntosh, "The State and the Oppression of Women," in *Feminism and Materialism: Women and Modes of Production*, ed. Annette Kuhn and Ann Marie Wolpe (Boston: Routledge & Kegan Paul, 1978), pp. 254–289.

24. Elizabeth Wilson, *Women and the Welfare State* (London: Tavistock, 1977), p. 9.

CHAPTER FOUR   Consumer Bodies

1. *The Republic of Plato*, Bk. II, 372A, tr. F. M. Cornford (Oxford: Clarendon Press, 1941).

2. John Kenneth Galbraith, *The Affluent Society* (Boston: Houghton Mifflin, 1958), p. 153. See also my "Public and Private Space," in *Sociology as a Skin Trade*, pp. 20–37.

3. See Michael Oakeshott, "Moral Life in the Writings of Thomas Hobbes," in his *Rationalism in Politics and Other Essays* (London: Methuen, 1967); also Albert O. Hirschman, *The Passions and the Interests: Political Arguments for Capitalism before Its Triumph* (Princeton: Princeton University Press, 1977).

4. Bernard Mandeville, *The Fable of the Bees*, ed. Phillip Harth (Harmondsworth: Penguin Books, 1970), Preface, pp. 54–55.

5. For a critical Marxist review of *The Theory of the Leisure Class* see Paul A. Baran, *The Longer View: Essays toward a Critique of Political Economy*, ed. with an introduction by John O'Neill (New York: Monthly Review Press, 1969), pp. 210–222.

6. Ruth Benedict, *Patterns of Culture* (London: Routledge & Kegan Paul, 1935).

7. Mary Douglas and Baron Isherwood, *The World of Goods: Towards an Anthropology of Consumption* (London: Allen Lane: 1979), chap. 7, "Separate Economic Spheres in Ethnography."

8. See Marvin Harris, "Potlatch," in his *Cows, Pigs, Wars and Witches*, pp. 81–97. See also William Leiss, "Needs, Exchanges and the Fetishism of Objects," *Canadian Journal of Political and Social Theory*, 2 (Fall 1978), 27–48; and Vance Packard, *The Status Seekers* (New York: McKay, 1959).

9. Henri Lefebvre, "The Bureaucratic Society of Controlled Consumption," in his *Everyday Life in the Modern World*, tr. Sacha Rabinovitch (London: Allen Lane, 1971), pp. 102–103.

10. Roland Barthes, "The New Citroën," in his *Mythologies*, selected and tr. Annette Lavette (London: Paladin, 1973), p. 88.

11. Jean Baudrillard, *Pour une critique de l'économie politique du signe* (Paris: Gallimard, 1972), pp. 76–77. Compare Harvey Cox's analysis of the functions of Miss America and Playboy in his *The Secular City: Secularization and Urbanization in Theological Perspective* (New York: Macmillan, 1971), pp. 167–178.

12. For an analysis of Marx's understanding of the categories of production and consumption in the *Grundrisse*, see Roslyn Wallach Bol-

ogh, *Dialectical Phenomenology: Marx's Method* (London: Routledge & Kegan Paul, 1979), pp. 61–69.

13. See Marshall Sahlins, "La pensée bourgeoise: Western Society as Culture," in his *Culture and Practical Reason*, pp. 166–204.

14. Sennett and Cobb, *Hidden Injuries of Class*, p. 171.

15. John Kenneth Galbraith, "Consumption and the Concept of the Household," in his *Economics and the Public Purpose* (Boston: Houghton Mifflin, 1973), pp. 31–40.

16. Galbraith, "Consumption," pp. 39–40.

17. Galbraith, "The Equitable Household and Beyond," *Economics and the Public Purpose*, pp. 253–261.

18. See Arthur L. Caplan, *The Sociobiology Debate* (New York: Harper & Row, 1978).

19. Juliet Mitchell, "Women: The Longest Revolution," *New Left Review*, November-December 1966, pp. 11–37.

20. Alice S. Rossi, "Maternalism, Sexuality, and the New Feminism," in *Contemporary Sexual Behavior: Critical Issues in the 1970's*, ed. Joseph Zubin and John Money (Baltimore: Johns Hopkins University Press, 1973), p. 169.

21. René Levy, "Psychosomatic Symptoms and Women's Protest: Two Types of Reaction to Structural Strain in the Family," *Journal of Health and Social Behavior*, 17 (June 1976), 122–134.

22. Lionel Trilling, "The Kinsey Report," in his *The Liberal Imagination: Essays on Literature and Society* (New York: Viking, 1950), p. 242.

CHAPTER FIVE   Medical Bodies

1. Vicente Navarro, "Social Class, Political Power, and the State: Their Implications in Medicine," in *Critical Sociology: European Perspectives*, ed. J. W. Freiberg (New York: Irvington, 1979), pp. 297–344.

2. See Ivan Illich, "Tantalizing Needs," in his *Toward a History of Needs* (New York: Pantheon, 1977), pp. 93–94; also Ivan Illich, *Medical Nemesis: The Expropriation of Health* (London: Calder & Boyars, 1975); and Vicente Navarro, "The Industrialization of Fetishism or the Fetishism of Industrialization: A Critique of Ivan Illich," *Social Science and Medicine*, 9 (1975), 351–363; also David F. Horrobin, *Medical Hubris: A Reply to Ivan Illich* (Montreal: Eden Press, 1977).

3. *Work in America: Report of a Special Task Force to the Secretary of*

Health, Education and Welfare (Cambridge: M.I.T. Press, 1973), pp. 77–79.

4. Peter K. Manning and Horacio Fabrega, Jr., "The Experience of Self and Body: Health and Illness in the Chiapas Highlands," in *Phenomenological Sociology: Issues and Applications*, ed. George Psathas, copyright © 1973 by John Wiley and Sons, Inc. (New York: Wiley, 1973), pp. 251–301. Reprinted by permission of the publisher.

5. Illich, *Medical Nemesis*, p. 160.

6. Richard M. Titmuss, *The Gift Relationship: From Human Blood to Social Policy* (New York: Vintage, 1971); see also G. E. W. Wolstenholme, "An Old Established Procedure: The Development of Blood Transfusion," in *Ethics in Medical Progress, with Special Reference to Transplantation*, ed. G. E. W. Wolstenholme and Maeve O'Connor (London: J. and A. Churchill, 1966), pp. 24–42.

7. See Irene Taviss, "Problems in the Social Control of Biomedical Science and Technology," in *Human Aspects of Biomedical Innovation*, ed. Everett Mendelsohn, Judith P. Swazey, and Irene Taviss (Cambridge: Harvard University Press, 1971), pp. 3–45.

8. See Gerald Leach, *The Biocrats: Implications of Medical Progress* (Harmondsworth: Penguin, 1972); also Amitai Etzioni, *Genetic Fix: The Next Technological Revolution* (New York: Harper Colophon, 1973).

9. Titmuss, *Gift Relationship*, p. 158.

10. Jonathan Miller, *The Body in Question* (London: Jonathan Cape, 1978), chap. 6, "The Amiable Juice."

11. Miller, *Body in Question*, chap. 8, "Is the Gift a Good One?"

12. Titmuss, *Gift Relationship*, pp. 245–246.

13. Etzioni, *Genetic Fix*, 104. This book is copyright © 1973 by Amitai Etzioni, and the table is reproduced by permission of the Macmillan Publishing Company.

14. Titmuss, *Gift Relationship*, chap. 13, "Who Is My Stranger?"

15. Titmuss, *Gift Relationship*, pp. 225–226.

16. See Alan Sheridan, *Michel Foucault: The Will to Truth*. London: Tavistock, 1980).

17. Michel Foucault, *Discipline and Punish: The Birth of the Prison*, tr. Alan Sheridan (New York: Vintage, 1979), p. 28.

18. Foucault, *History of Sexuality*, I:45. First emphasis mine.

19. Foucault, *History of Sexuality*, I:98–102.

20. Foucault, *History of Sexuality*, I:146–147. My emphasis.

21. See Donzelot, *The Policing of Families*.

22. Nicholas N. Kittrie, *The Right to Be Different: Deviance and Enforced*

Therapy (Baltimore: Johns Hopkins Press, 1971), especially chap. 8, "The Therapeutic Ideal: The Evils of Unchecked Power."

23. Kittrie, *Right to Be Different*, pp. 392–393. My emphasis.

24. Philip Rieff, *The Triumph of the Therapeutic: Uses of Faith after Freud* (London: Chatto & Windus, 1966), p. 61.

25. Rieff, *Triumph of the Therapeutic*, p. 65.

26. Rieff, *Triumph of the Therapeutic*, p. 26.

27. See Nanette J. Davis and Bo Anderson, *Social Control: The Production of Deviance in the Modern State* (New York: Irvington, 1983).

28. Rieff, *Triumph of the Therapeutic*, pp. 24–25.

29. Ewen, *Captains of Consciousness*, pp. 201–202.

30. James Agee and Walker Evans, *Let Us Now Praise Famous Men* (New York: Ballantine, 1966), p. 52.

CONCLUSION   The Future Shape of Human Being

1. Dylan Thomas, "Was There a Time," *Collected Poems, 1934–1952* (London: Dent, 1952), p. 50.

2. Vico, *The New Science*, para. 377.

3. Vico, *The New Science*, para. 520.

4. Vico, *The New Science*, para. 374.

5. See Foucault, *Discipline and Punish*, and *History of Sexuality*.

6. See Aubrey Milunsky and George J. Annas, eds., *Genetics and the Law*, vols. I and II (New York: Plenum Press, 1975 and 1980).

7. Leach, *The Biocrats*, pp. 153–154, my emphasis.

8. See Jean Baudrillard, *De la séduction* (Paris: Galilée, 1979), pp. 231–232.

9. See Illich, *Medical Nemesis*; also Ivan Illich, *The Cultural Crisis of Modern Medicine*, ed. John Ehrenreich (New York: Monthly Review Press, 1978).

10. Thomas, *Collected Poems*, p. 116.

BIBLIOGRAPHY

Archambault, Paul. "The Analogy of the 'Body' in Renaissance Political Literature." *Bibliothèque d'Humanisme et Renaissance*, 29 (1967), 21–63.

Baldwin, B. A. "Behavioural Thermoregulation." In *Heat Loss from Animals and Man: Assessment and Control*. Ed. J. I. Monteith and L. E. Mount. London: Butterworth, 1974. Pp. 97–117.

Baran, Paul A. *The Longer View: Essays toward a Critique of Political Economy*. Ed. with an introduction by John O'Neill. New York: Monthly Review Press, 1969.

Barkan, Leonard. *Nature's Work of Art: The Human Body as Image of the World*. New Haven: Yale University Press, 1975.

Barthes, Roland. *Mythologies*. Selected and tr. Annette Lavette. London: Paladin, 1973.

Baudrillard, Jean. *De la séduction*. Paris: Galilée, 1979.

——. *Pour une critique de l'économie politique du signe*. Paris: Gallimard, 1972.

Benedict, Ruth. *Patterns of Culture*. London: Routledge & Kegan Paul, 1935.

Berman, Morris. *The Reenchantment of the World*. Ithaca: Cornell University Press, 1981.

Bledstein, Burton J. *The Culture of Professionalism: The Middle Class and the Development of Higher Education in America*. New York: Norton, 1978.

Blumer, Ralph. "Why Is the Cassowary not a Bird? A Problem of Zoo-

logical Taxonomy among the Karam of the New Guinea Highlands."
Man, n.s. 2 (March 1967), 5–25.

Bologh, Roslyn Wallach. *Dialectical Phenomenology: Marx's Method*. London: Routledge & Kegan Paul, 1979.

Borgstrom, George. *The Food and People Dilemma*. Belmont, Calif.: Duxbury Press, 1973.

Bourdieu, Pierre. "Remarques provisoires sur la perception sociale du corps." *Actes de la Recherche en Sciences Sociales*, April 14, 1977. Pp. 51–54.

Brophy, Julia, and Carol Smart. "From Disregard to Disrepute: The Position of Women in Family Law." *Feminist Review*, 9 (1981), 3–15.

Busaca, Richard, and Mary P. Ryan. "Beyond the Family Crisis", *Democracy*, 2 (Fall 1982), 79–92.

Calame-Griaule, Geneviève. *Ethnologie et languge: La parole chez les Dogon*. Paris: Gallimard, 1965.

Caplan, Arthur L. *The Sociobiology Debate*. New York: Harper & Row, 1978.

Clark, Carole. "Montaigne and the Imagery of Political Discourse in Sixteenth Century France." *French Studies*, 24 (October 1970), 337–355.

Cockburn, Alexander. "Gastro-Porn." *The New York Review of Books*, December 8, 1977. Pp. 15–19.

Conger, George Perrigo. *Theories of Macrocosms and Microcosms*. New York: Columbia University Press, 1922.

Cooley, Charles Horton. *Human Nature and the Social Order*. New York: Schocken, 1964.

Cox, Harvey. *The Secular City: Secularization and Urbanization in Theological Perspective*. New York: Macmillan, 1971.

Crawford, M. A., and J. P. W. Rivers. "The Protein Myth." In *The Man/Food Equation*. Ed. F. Steele and A. Bourne. New York: Academic Press, 1975. Pp. 235–245.

Davis, Nanette J., and Bo Anderson. *Social Control: The Production of Deviance in the Modern State*. New York: Irvington, 1983.

Diener, Paul, and Eugene E. Robkin. "Ecology, Evolution, and the Search for Cultural Origins: The Question of Islamic Pig Production." *Current Anthropology*, 19 (September 1978), 493–540.

Donzelot, Jacques. *The Policing of Families*. Tr. Robert Hurley. New York: Pantheon, 1979.

Douglas, Mary. "Cultural Bias." London: Royal Anthropological Institute of Great Britain and Ireland, Occasional Paper no. 35, 1978.

——. *Implicit Meanings: Essays in Anthropology*. London: Routledge & Kegan Paul, 1975.

——. *Natural Symbols: Explorations in Cosmology*. Harmondsworth: Penguin, 1973.

——. *Purity and Danger: An Analysis of Concepts of Pollution and Taboo*. Harmondsworth: Penguin Books, 1970.

——. *Rules and Meanings: The Anthropology of Everyday Knowledge*. Harmondsworth: Penguin, 1973.

Douglas, Mary, and Baron Isherwood. *The World of Goods: Towards an Anthropology of Consumption*. London: Allen Lane, 1979.

Durkheim, Emile, and Marcel Mauss. *Primitive Classification*. Tr. and ed. with an introduction by Rodney Needham. London: Cohen & West, 1963.

Eliade, Mircea. *The Forge and the Crucible: The Origins and Structures of Alchemy*. Tr. Stephen Corrin. 2d ed. Chicago: University of Chicago Press, 1978.

Elshtain, Jean Bethke. *Public Man, Private Woman: Women in Social and Political Thought*. Oxford: Martin Robertson, 1981.

Etzioni, Amitai. *Genetic Fix: The Next Technological Revolution*. New York: Harper Colophon, 1973.

Ewen, Stuart. *Captains of Consciousness: Advertising and the Social Roots of the Consumer Culture*. New York: McGraw-Hill, 1976.

Fortescue, Sir John. *De laudibus Legum Angliae*. Ed. and tr. with introduction and notes by S.B. Chrimes. Cambridge: Cambridge University Press, 1949.

Foucault, Michel. *Discipline and Punish: The Birth of the Prison*. Tr. Alan Sheridan. New York: Vintage, 1979.

——. *The History of Sexuality*. Tr. Robert Hurley. New York: Vintage, 1980.

Freud, Sigmund. *Civilization and Its Discontents*. Tr. and ed. James Strachey. New York: Norton, 1962.

Frosch, Thomas R. *The Awakening of Albion: The Renovation of the Body in the Poetry of William Blake*. Ithaca: Cornell University Press, 1974.

Galbraith, John Kenneth. *Economics and the Public Purpose*. Boston: Houghton Mifflin, 1973.

——. *The Affluent Society*. Boston: Houghton Mifflin, 1958.

Gierke, Otto. *Political Theories of the Middle Age*. Tr. with introduction by F. W. Maitland. Cambridge: Cambridge University Press, 1958.

Grene, Marjorie. *Approaches to Philosophical Biology*. New York: Basic, 1965.

Griaule, Marcel. *Conversations with Ogotommêli: An Introduction to Dogon Religious Ideas*. London: Oxford University Press, 1965.

Habermas, Jürgen. *Legitimation Crisis*. Tr. Thomas McCarthy. Boston: Beacon, 1975.

Hacker, Andrew. "Farewell to the Family?" *The New York Review of Books*, March 18, 1982. Pp. 37–44.

Harris, Marvin. *Cannibals and Kings*. London: Fontana, 1978.

——. "Cannibals and Kings: An Exchange." *The New York Review of Books*, June 28, 1979. Pp. 51–53.

——. *Cows, Pigs, Wars and Witches: The Riddles of Culture*. London: Fontana, 1977.

Hertz, Robert. *Death and the Right Hand*. Tr. Rodney and Claudia Needham. Glencoe, Ill.: Free Press, 1960.

Hirschman, Albert O. *The Passions and the Interests: Political Arguments for Capitalism before Its Triumph*. Princeton: Princeton University Press, 1977.

Horrobin, David F. *Medical Hubris: A Reply to Ivan Illich*. Montreal: Eden Press, 1977.

Illich, Ivan. *The Cultural Crisis of Modern Medicine*. Ed. John Ehrenreich. New York: Monthly Review Press, 1978.

——. *Gender*. New York: Pantheon, 1982.

——. *Medical Nemesis: The Expropriation of Health*. London: Calder & Boyars, 1975.

——. *Toward a History of Needs*. New York: Pantheon, 1977.

Kantorowicz, Ernst. *The King's Two Bodies*. Princeton: Princeton University Press, 1957.

Kittrie, Nicholas N. *The Right to Be Different: Deviance and Enforced Therapy*. Baltimore: Johns Hopkins Press, 1971.

Lappé, Frances Moore. *Diet for a Small Planet*. New York: Ballantine, 1975.

Lasch, Christopher. "Life in the Therapeutic State." *The New York Review of Books*, June 12, 1980. Pp. 24–32.

Leach, Edmund. "Anthropological Aspects of Language: Animal Categories and Verbal Abuse." In *New Directions in the Study of Language*. Ed. Eric H. Lenneberg. Cambridge: MIT Press, 1964. Pp. 23–63.

——. *Claude Lévi-Strauss*. New York: Viking, 1970.

——. "Genesis as Myth." In *Myth and Cosmos: Readings in Mythology and Symbolism*. Ed. John Middleton. Garden City, N.Y.: Natural History Press, 1967. Pp. 1–13.

Leach, Gerald. *The Biocrats: Implications of Medical Progress*. Harmondsworth: Penguin, 1972.

Lebeuf, Jean-Paul. *L'habitation des Fali: Montagnards du Cameroun septentrional*. Paris: Hachette, 1961.

Lefebvre, Henri. *Everyday Life in the Modern World*. Tr. Sacha Rabinovitch. London: Allen Lane, 1971.

Leiss, William. "Needs, Exchanges and the Fetishism of Objects." *Canadian Journal of Political and Social Theory*, 2 (Fall 1978), 27–48.

Lévi-Strauss, Claude. *The Raw and the Cooked: Introduction to a Science of Mythology*. vol. 1. Tr. John and Doreen Weightman. New York: Harper & Row, 1970.

——. *The Savage Mind*. Chicago: University of Chicago Press, 1966.

——. "Le triangle culinaire." *L'Arc*, no. 26 (1965), pp. 19–29.

Levy, René. "Psychosomatic Symptoms and Women's Protest: Two Types of Reaction to Structural Strain in the Family." *Journal of Health and Social Behavior*, 17 (June 1976), 122–134.

MacRae, Donald G. "The Body and Social Metaphor." In *The Body as a Medium of Expression: An Anthology*. Ed. with an introduction by Jonathan Benthall and Ted Polhemus. New York: Dutton, 1975. Pp. 59–73.

Manning, Peter K., and Horacio Fabrega, Jr. "The Experience of Self and Body: Health and Illness in the Chiapas Highlands." In *Phenomenological Sociology: Issues and Applications*. Ed. George Psathas. New York: Wiley, 1973. Pp. 251–301.

Marmorstein, Arthur. *The Old Rabbinic Doctrine of God, II. Essays in Anthropomorphism*. Oxford: Oxford University Press, 1937.

Mauss, Marcel. "Techniques of the Body." *Economy and Society*, 2, (1973), 70–88.

McIntosh, Mary. "The State and the Oppression of Women." In *Feminism and Materialism: Women and Modes of Production*. Ed. Annette Kuhn and Ann Marie Wolpe. Boston: Routledge & Kegan Paul, 1978. Pp. 254–289.

Merleau-Ponty, Maurice. *Phenomenology of Perception*. Tr. Colin Smith. London: Routledge & Kegan Paul, 1962.

Miller, Jonathan. *The Body in Question*. London: Jonathan Cape, 1978.

Milunsky, Aubrey and George J. Annas, ed. *Genetics and the Law*, I and II. New York: Plenum Press, 1975 and 1980.

Mitchell, Juliet. "Women: The Longest Revolution." *New Left Review*, November-December 1966. Pp. 11–37.

Navarro, Vicente. "The Industrialization of Fetishism or the Fetishism of Industrialization: A Critique of Ivan Illich." *Social Science and Medicine*, 9 (1975), 351–363.

——. "Social Class, Political Power and the State: Their Implications in Medicine." In *Critical Sociology: European Perspectives*. Ed. J. W. Freiberg. New York: Irvington, 1979. Pp. 297–344.

Oakeshott, Michael. *Rationalism in Politics and Other essays*. London: Methuen, 1967.

O'Neill, John. "Critique and Remembrance", In *On Critical Theory*. Ed. John O'Neill. New York: Seabury, 1976. Pp. 1–11.

——. "Defamilization and the Feminization of Law in Early and Late Capitalism." *International Journal of Law and Psychiatry*, 5 (1982), 255–269.

——. "Embodiment and Child Development: A Phenomenological Approach." In *Recent Sociology No. 5: Childhood and Socialization*. Ed. Hans Peter Dreitzel. New York: Macmillan, 1973. Pp. 65–81. Reprinted in *The Sociology of Childhood: Essential Readings*. Ed. Chris Jenks. London: Batsford, 1982. Pp. 76–86.

——. "Lecture visuelle de l'espace urbain." In *Colloque d'esthetique appliquée à la création du paysage urbain: Collection presenté par Michel Conan*. Paris: Copedith, 1975. Pp. 235–247.

——. "Looking into the Media: Revelation and Subversion." In *Communication Philosophy and the Technological Age*. Ed. Michael J. Hyde. University: University of Alabama Press, 1982. Pp. 73–97.

——. *Making Sense Together: An Introduction to Wild Sociology*. New York: Harper & Row, 1974.

——. "On Simmel's 'Sociological Apriorities.'" *Phenomenological Sociology: Issues and Applications*. Ed. George Psathas. New York: Wiley, 1973. Pp. 91–106.

——. *Perception, Expression and History*. Evanston: Northwestern University Press, 1970.

——. *Sociology as a Skin Trade, Essays towards a Reflexive Sociology*. New York: Harper & Row, 1972.

——. "Time's Body: Vico on the Love of Language and Institution." In *Giambattista Vico's Science of Humanity*. Ed. Giorgio Tagliacozza and Donald Phillip Verene. Baltimore: Johns Hopkins University Press, 1976. Pp. 333–339.

Packard, Vance. *The Status Seekers*. New York: 1959.

Rank, Otto. *Art and Artist: Creative Urge and Personality Development*. Tr. Charles Francis Atkinson. New York: Agathon Press, 1968.

Rieff, Philip. *The Triumph of the Therapeutic: Uses of Faith after Freud.* London: Chatto & Windus, 1966.

Robinson, John A. T. *The Body: A Study in Pauline Theology.* London: SCM Press, 1952.

Rossi, Alice. S. "Maternalism, Sexuality and the New Feminism." In *Contemporary Sexual Behaviour: Critical Issues in the 1970's.* Ed. Joseph Zubin and John Money. Baltimore: Johns Hopkins University Press, 1973.

Sahlins, Marshall, "Cannibalism: An Exchange." *The New York Review of Books,* March 22, 1979. Pp. 45–47.

———. *Culture and Practical Reason.* Chicago: University of Chicago Press, 1976.

———. "Culture as Protein and Profit." *The New York Review of Books,* November 23, 1978. Pp. 45–53.

Sennett, Richard, and Jonathan Cobb. *The Hidden Injuries of Class.* New York: Vintage, 1973.

Sheridan, Alan. *Michel Foucault: The Will to Truth.* London: Tavistock, 1980.

Soler, Jean. "The Dietary Prohibitions of the Hebrews," *The New York Review of Books,* June 14, 1979. Pp. 24–30.

Tambiah, S. J. "Animals Are Good to Think and Good to Prohibit." *Ethnology,* 8 (October 1969), 424–459.

Taviss, Irene, "Problems in the Social Control of Biomedical Science and Technology." In *Human Aspects of Biomedical Innovation.* Ed. Everett Mendelsohn, Judith P. Swazey, and Irene Taviss. Cambridge: Harvard University Press, 1971. Pp. 3–45.

Titmuss, Richard M. *The Gift Relationship: From Human Blood to Social Policy.* New York: Vintage, 1971.

Trilling, Lionel. *The Liberal Imagination: Essays on Literature and Society.* New York: Viking, 1950.

Turner, Victor. *Dramas, Fields, and Metaphors: Symbolic Action in Human Society.* Ithaca: Cornell University Press, 1974.

———. "The Word of the Dogon." *Social Science Information,* 7 (1968), 55–61.

Veblen, Thorstein. *The Theory of the Leisure Class.* London: Allen & Unwin, 1925.

The New Science of Giambattista Vico. Tr. from the third edition by Thomas Goddard Bergin and Max Harold Fisch. Ithaca: Cornell University Press, 1970.

Wilson, Elizabeth. *Women and the Welfare State.* London: Tavistock, 1977.

Wolstenholme, G.E.W. "An Old Established Procedure: The Development of Blood Transfusion." In *Ethics in Medical Progress, with Special Reference to Transplantation*. Ed. G.E.W. Wolstenholme and Maeve O'Connor. London: J. and A. Churchill, 1966. Pp. 24–42.

Work in America: Report of a Special Task Force to the Secretary of Health, Education, and Welfare. Cambridge: MIT Press, 1973. Pp. 77–79.

INDEX

Library of Congress Cataloging in Publication Data

O'Neill, John, 1933–
    Five bodies.

    Bibliography: p.
    Includes index.
    1. Body, Human—Social aspects. 2. Social structure. 3. Religion and
sociology. 4. Social problems. I. Title.
GN298.054   1985   573'.6   84-22947
ISBN 0-8014-1727-9 (alk. paper)